Striking Terror No More

This is my hand
     that no one will hold.
Like the rest of me
     it hurts and feels terribly cold.
I want you to hold it,
     But I am so scared
You'll be like the others
     For no one has cared.

At the chronological age of 37 years, I am being born! In that birth, I am discovering *for the first time* that life and the world are very different from anything I have ever known. . . . The most amazing thing to me and the thing I want to share with you is that I have discovered in my infancy today that *I am a treasure!*

O LORD, you will hear the desire of the meek;
     you will strengthen their heart,
          you will incline your ear
to do justice for the orphan and the oppressed,
     so that those from earth may
          strike terror no more.

—Psalm 10:17–18

I cannot forget about what was
     done to me.
I must do what I must so that
     others may see
     "anything that is done in
          darkness will come to light."
My shining light is but a glimmer
     of hope
     because it's me that must cope.
I am pressing forward.
I'm getting the help that I need.
And one day justice will triumph
     over one man's evil deeds.

If you should ever again
     See this pain on a face
Or see a cold hand
     Outstretched in some place,
Take hold of that hand,
     Of yourself try to give.
You'll be better knowing
     You've helped a child live.

Striking Terror No More

The Church Responds to Domestic Violence

Edited by Beth Basham and Sara Lisherness

Bridge Resources
Louisville, Kentucky

The editors wish to thank Family and Children's Agency of Louisville, Kentucky, for providing personal accounts of family violence in narrative, poetic, and pictorial forms from its client population for use in this resource.

Unless otherwise noted, Scripture quotations are from the New Revised Standard Version of the Bible, copyright © 1989 by the Division of Christian Education of the National Council of the Churches of Christ in the U.S.A. Used by permission.

Every effort has been made to trace copyrights on the materials included in this book. If any copyrighted material has nevertheless been included without permission and due acknowledgment, proper credit will be inserted in future printings after notice has been received.

Editors

Beth Basham, Senior Acquisitions Editor, Curriculum Publishing Program Area, Presbyterian Church (U.S.A.)
Sara Lisherness, Associate, Presbyterian Peacemaking Program Area, Presbyterian Church (U.S.A.)

Project Assistants

Connie Ellis, Administrative Assistant, Editorial Program Team, Curriculum Publishing Program Area, Presbyterian Church (U.S.A.)
Sonja Ward, Administrative Assistant, Presbyterian Peacemaking Program Area, Presbyterian Church (U.S.A.)

Book interior and cover design by Anthony Feltner

First edition

Bridge Resources
Louisville, Kentucky
PRINTED IN THE UNITED STATES OF AMERICA

http://www.pcusa.org/pcusa/currpub

Library of Congress Cataloging-in-Publication Data

Striking terror no more : the church responds to domestic violence /
    edited by Beth Basham and Sara Lisherness. — 1st ed.
          p.   cm.
    Includes bibliographical references.
    ISBN 1-57895-014-7
    1. Church work with abused women. 2. Family violence—Religious aspects—Christianity.
I. Basham, Beth, date. II. Lisherness, Sara, date.
BV4445.5.S78   1997
261.8'327—dc21
97-10417

Contents

Foreword vii

Introduction ix

Part 1 Background Articles

Devisings of the Human Heart: The Bible and Violence 1
 Johanna W. H. van Wijk-Bos

We Won't Let It Happen Here: Keeping Children Safe from Sexual Abuse 8
 Lois Rifner

No Means No: Acquaintance Rape and Date Rape 11
 Andrea Parrot

Picking Up the Broken Pieces: Responding to Domestic Violence 13
 Marie M. Fortune

Ageing and Ageism: Implications for the Church's Ministry with Families 20
 Thomas B. Robb

Part 2 Suggested Workshops

What Is Domestic Violence Anyway? 31

Child Abuse 35

Acquaintance Rape and Date Rape 45

Spouse Abuse 53

Elder Abuse 69

Part 3 Worship Resources 83

Appendix A 101

Appendix B 112

Suggested Resources 117

Foreword

In 1995 the General Assembly Council of the Presbyterian Church (U.S.A.) developed a new program initiative to address the violence in our society, specifically violence against women. The Societal Violence Team was called together to find creative ways of focusing the church's attention on the women and girls in their pews and communities who are victims of violence. Many team members have expertise in the field of violence and violence against women.

"The church is not a safe place," she said. "I didn't feel I could go there for help." These were the words the members of the team heard during a visit to a shelter for battered women and children in Louisville, Kentucky. These words have given direction to the team's work.

With a mission of raising awareness, promoting education, and empowering women and men to make changes in their churches and communities, a comprehensive resource packet has been produced that includes this piece, *Striking Terror No More: The Church Responds to Domestic Violence*. We are pleased that a joint effort of Women's Ministries, Health Ministries, Bridge Resources of the Curriculum Publishing Program Area, and the Presbyterian Peacemaking Program has brought this excellent piece to life. We are also grateful for the contributions of Johanna W. H. van Wijk-Bos, Marie M. Fortune, Katie Jacobs, Andrea Parrot, Rebecca Todd Peters, Lois Rifner, Thomas B. Robb, and Susan Smith. This resource addresses the violence experienced at all ages—childhood through older adulthood. It helps us understand the many forms of violence prevalent in our church and society. Most important, it calls us to change our attitudes and actions, to be a faithful people who care for those in need.

It is our hope and prayer that the information contained in this resource, when shared with women and men, boys and girls, will help us to move forward in the struggle to make the church "a safe, caring place" for all and a leader in seeking justice and nonviolence within our communities.

Kristine K. Thompson
on behalf of the Societal Violence Initiative Team

Introduction

In the approximately two minutes it will take you to read this introduction, at least eight women will be severely injured in their homes by their husbands or boyfriends. Think about it—in approximately two minutes, at least eight women.

In the United States, violence against women in the home causes more injuries than rape, muggings, and car accidents combined.

- Approximately 95 percent of the victims of domestic violence are women.
- An estimated 25–50 percent of all women will be physically assaulted in an intimate relationship.
- Three to four million women in the United States are battered every year by their husbands or partners.
- In over half of the homes where women are being battered, their children are being abused as well.

Violence in the family—physical assault, psychological abuse, sexual abuse, and destruction of property—is a national crisis. It is also a crisis in our faith communities.

"In the pews of every church every Sunday sit both perpetrators and their victims. They come from all racial and ethnic groups, can be wealthy, middle class, or poor, lawyers or teachers, business people or construction workers. They are Presbyterian, Catholic, Lutheran, Baptist, Church of God in Christ, Unitarian, AME Methodist—in every denomination in the United States."[1]

However, also among us every Sunday are survivors of violence in the families. Without their courage to tell their stories and to name the violence, this resource would not be in your hands. Take a moment to lift up in thanksgiving the survivors in your midst whether you know them or not. They are present in every community; they are present in every congregation.

Churches can be a resource to those who are the victims or the perpetrators of violence. Yet, silence, ignorance, lack of skills, and denial to recognize the suffering of congregants who are victims of violence continues. There are some of us who still believe that obedience to the Scriptures means that wives must "submit" to their husbands, which is often interpreted as the husband and father is to be the absolute head of the household and that "his" wife and children must obey him without question. What this has often resulted in is that wives and children must also submit to abuse from husbands and fathers. All faith communities must make it known that there is *nothing* in Christian teachings that justifies abuse or violence against another person.

If "the sparrow finds a home, and the swallow a nest for herself, where she may lay her young, at [God's] altar" (Ps. 84:3), then women and children running away from violence in their families should find their churches a sanctuary for safety and refuge. It is time for the church to reclaim its role as a sanctuary for those in danger of further harm. A victim must be able to know without doubt that she can turn to the church for help. The church must be a safe place for victims to name the truth of the violence in their lives. It must be a place where their truth is heard with solidarity and compassion. It must be a place where their reality is named at

---

[1] Reprinted by permission from *Woman Battering* by Carol J. Adams, copyright © 1994 Augsburg Fortress, p. 11.

the pulpit and where perpetrators are called to account. It must be a place of hope where they can begin to find justice and healing.

This study guide faithfully and clearly outlines how clergy and laity can learn the nature and causes of violence in the families and use the resources of our tradition appropriately to provide safety for the victims, to stop the abuse by calling the perpetrator to account, to restore relationship if possible, and if not, to mourn the loss of relationship. When violence is introduced in a relationship, the church cannot ignore it, hoping that the family can work it out and stay together. Everyone must work toward providing safety for the victims over keeping the family together. We must change our mindset that divorce is not what breaks a relationship. Relationship is broken long before the divorce actually happens. And violence, not a woman's decision to leave, breaks a relationship.

The church is called to confess its failure in the past to address this crisis effectively. The church is called to act on what it believes—that women and children are created in the image of God and that violence against them is a sin.

Our calling is to model in our families and in our churches the alternative to violence: sanctuaries of abundant life, safety, love, respect, and support for all.

The Reverend Thelma B. Burgonio-Watson
Member, Societal Violence Initiative Team
Presbyterian Church (U.S.A.)
Program Specialist: Center for the Prevention of Sexual and Domestic Violence
Seattle, Washington

Part 1

Background Articles

O LORD, you will hear the desire of the meek;
  you will strengthen their heart,
    you will incline your ear
to do justice for the orphan and the oppressed,
  so that those from earth may strike terror no more.
—*Psalm 10:17–18*

Devisings of the Human Heart:
The Bible and Violence

Johanna W. H. van Wijk-Bos

What is a biblical approach to human violence? Where is violence found in the human community and how do the biblical writers deal with it? In this overview, we will survey violence in the Bible from three perspectives. First, we look at texts that reflect overt forms of violence, acts of aggression on an individual and communal level. Second, we consider more hidden forms of violence, such as poverty and other types of discrimination, that occur as a result of particular societal structures. Finally, we focus on the recipients of violence.

At every point, we address the question of God's response to human violence as well as human responsibility. This review is carried out with the expectation that the biblical text will provide patterns that verify contemporary predicaments and at the same time furnish hope for liberation from these patterns.

"The Voice of Your Brother's Blood"

The Bible presents a clear view of human interaction as full of potential for violence and of the actual execution of it. In the myths that describe the construction of human society told in the first ten chapters of Genesis, the emphasis in terms of violence is on overt destructive action. The first time that the word *sin* occurs in these chapters is in the story of kin-slaughter of Abel by Cain. "Sin" is not introduced in the story of the garden. There, the humans were disobedient to the instructions laid down for them by God and faced the consequences of what they had done. Overall, the consequences of the act of disobedience can be classified as alienation: humanity will henceforth live an alienated existence in terms of the whole created world—animal, natural, and human (Gen. 2—3). This alienation is described as an ongoing process of deterioration in Gen. 4—10, until "God saw that the evil of humanity was great on earth and that all the devisings of its mind were only evil all the day" (Gen. 6:5).[1] For "the earth was a ruin before God and the earth was filled with violence" (Gen. 6:11). The latter phrase is repeated once when God announces to Noah the divine plan to wipe out most of the creation and to make a new beginning for the human family with Noah (Gen. 6:13).

Literally, the phrasing of v. 5 in Gen. 6 locates evil in the imagination: "every form of the planning of their heart was only evil all the day." Violence is the result of planned evil. It does not happen accidentally. Or, if it takes place by accident, it is not of the same category as the violence that fills the earth in the Genesis story. Because we may find the idea of a God who plans to destroy humanity repugnant or "primitive," the profundity of the observations about evil and violence may escape us. Yet, it is clear from this text that the biblical writers viewed violence as directly opposed to God's intentions for the creation.

The first recorded act of individual violence is from brother to brother, motivated by envy. In Gen. 4, as in ch. 6, the mental posture of the one who contemplates violence is emphasized. In God's interaction with Cain, the word *sin* falls for the first time when God asks

---

[1] All Scripture quotations are the author's translation unless otherwise noted.

Cain why his face is downcast and warns him that sin crouches at the door but that he can rule it (Gen. 4:7). When Cain has perpetrated his violent act, God exclaims: "What have you done? The voice of the blood of your brother cries to me from the ground" (Gen. 4:10). In other words, the violence done to Abel demands God's attention. That God is not pleased appears from the sequel. Human violence is a matter for divine attention and punishment. Eventually the violence of the earth will so appall the Creator that God plans to make a new beginning since nothing good can come of the evil devisings of human creatures. Violence has taken root in the human imagination and dwells there permanently.

The folk of the Bible had no illusions about human nature, it appears. Historically, the faith community that created the biblical text was overly familiar with violence in terms of overt acts of aggression. Ancient Israel was located at the crossroads where empires met in their violent attempts to achieve dominion over that part of the world. When it finally succumbed to the militarism of the reigning power of Babylon in the sixth century B.C.E., it was not to establish itself again as an independent country until the latter part of the twentieth century C.E. Intimate acquaintance with aggression was the mark of the faith community in ancient times.

The beginnings of ancient Israel were marked by violence, and its creation as a covenant community took place in a framework of oppression. When the slaves suffered in Egypt, God noticed the violence done to "Israel's children." The text observes that God "saw" and "heard" and "knew" the woes of the people before the Egyptian slave drivers (Ex. 3:7). In line with this concern, God announced divine intervention on behalf of the slaves in Egypt through the agency of Moses. In their suffering the violence done to them, the people were to find the point of their identity so that they would not in their turn perpetrate the same kind of violence. Therefore, the directive in the Torah stipulates: "A stranger you must not oppress, you yourselves know the heart of the stranger, for you were strangers in the land of Egypt" (Ex. 23:9).

The entry into the land of the promise is told in the Bible as a violent affair. A disturbing note in the accounts of the so-called conquest is that the community viewed its actions as willed by God. (See Josh. 3:9–10; 8:1–2; 10:40, for example.) Yet, the military actions involved in the conquest were a part of ancient Israel's history rather than a motivation for renewed violence. Ancient Israel had no concept of holy war and was most of the time the victim rather than the perpetrator of the violence that constitutes war. We may consign the acts of aggression that are depicted in the book of Joshua to ancient stories—part history, part fiction—embellished as all such nationalistic accounts, but not designed as models for aggression.

God's reaction to overt human violence is generally depicted in the Bible as negative, and the Bible assumes that God intends *shalom*, peace or wholeness, for the human family. In the prophetic vision of the restored creation, the reality of war is a thing of the past. Swords and spears are turned into plowshares and pruning hooks, tools that prevail in peace time; no energy of imagination and mental process will be devoted to the study of war in that time (cf. Isa. 2:4). In Isa. 11:4–9, the prophet provides a picture of the healing of hostility between creature and creature and an end to evil doing and ruin: "they will not do evil and create ruin on all my holy mountain" (Isa. 11:9). And, in explicit counterpoint to Gen. 6:1–14, the earth will be filled with the knowledge of God rather than with violence (Isa. 11:9).

The word that most comprehensively and explicitly refers to human overt violence is *hamas* in Hebrew. This kind of violence is said to be "in the hands," to indicate its physical nature. Hands deal out *hamas* so that it can be tantamount to slaughter. Physical violence and brutality are certainly a part of *hamas*. In the third chapter of Jonah, the Ninevites, in order to complete their repentance process, have to let go of "the violence that is in their hands," a violence that definitely included the waging of war. Not until the Ninevites abandon their ways of bloodshed does God turn to them in mercy.

What ancient Israel saw, we see: violence in terms of hostile and aggressive activity, individual to individual and community to community, is a part of the human landscape. In terms of a biblical approach to this aspect of our existence, we can confidently say that God is not in accord with this type of violence, does not approve of it, faces folk with their responsibility for it, and envisions for the human community an existence without this dominant reality. In addition, people have a choice in terms of the exercise of violent action. Once violence is born in the imagination, it is still possible to control it (Gen. 4:7). Moreover, the story of Nineveh's repentance of its violence and God's subsequent change of heart furnishes an example of both the possibility and the power of such decision making.

The Practice of Violence

The absence of war does not guarantee the absence of violence. War is simply the most obvious form of violence. More often than not, the violence that occurs in the biblical records is the result of injustice from neighbor to neighbor. This kind of violence is less glamorous and therefore less obvious than the activity of war, but it is more consistently and severely denounced in the Scripture. Two common arenas for the practice of violence are the society and legal system.

In the society, violence is extended to the poor, the ones who have no resources, those who are consistently victimized by the rich. The community of ancient Israel was to model itself on a God who cared passionately for the plight of the poor. The prophets therefore speak sternly to the community against the violence perpetrated on this group. Amos, well known for holding the society accountable for divisions between rich and poor, accuses the well-to-do of bringing down "a reign of violence" on the poor (Amos 6:3 NRSV). Micah denounces dishonest practices of the wealthy and berates them for being "full of violence" (Mic. 6:12 NRSV).

Poverty is viewed in the Bible as a direct result of unjust structures. Where injustice prevails, oppression of the poor and the needy is the result, and this is seen as violence. The needy are equated with the righteous and the innocent. When these suffer oppression, the prophets denounce in the strongest possible terms the groups that deprive them and the community within which this deprivation occurs (cf. Amos 5:10–13). Justice and righteousness are those qualities that uphold the life of the weak and poor; injustice and unrighteousness are the marks of a society where those qualities are absent.

To deal justly and uphold the cause of the poor in the Bible is equated with the knowledge of God. In this respect, the leaders of the community are to set an example, and they are taken to task when they have failed to do so. In Jeremiah, the heirs of King Josiah, who live in luxury while laborers work for nothing and the innocent are deprived of life, are upbraided because of their lack of concern for the poor. "Are you a king because you compete in cedar?" the biblical writer asks sarcastically. "Did not your father eat and drink and do justice and righteousness? Then it was well with him. He judged the cause of the poor and needy; then it was well. Is not this to know me? says the LORD. But your eyes and heart are only on your dishonest gain, for shedding innocent blood; and for practicing oppression and violence" (Jer. 22:15–17 NRSV).

Conversely, the ideal ruler is the one who protects the poor and who defends their cause. Psalm 72 elaborately describes the actions of such a leader, who delivers the needy, has pity on the weak, and saves their life. "From oppression and violence he redeems their life; and precious is their blood in His sight" (Ps. 72:14). The same type of characterization is given to the servant of God in Isa. 40–55. The servant who will be a light to the nations and will bring them justice will not break a bruised reed, nor quench a smoldering wick (Isa. 42:1–4).

God is so opposed to the violence that victimizes the poor that the worship of a community that perpetrates this injustice is declared unacceptable. In text after text, the prophets attempt to convince the ancient covenant people of this truth. The violence of injustice so stains the community that everything they do is permeated with it. In a stark saying of Isaiah, the prophet declares that God has no pleasure in any of the rites of worship and also will not pay attention to the people's prayers as long as the same hands that they stretch out to God in prayer are "full of blood" (Isa. 1:15). Another passage has the community questioning the lack of attention God gives them, in view of their fervent fasting. The biblical writer then declares that this is not "a day acceptable to God." Rather, the acceptable fast consists of liberation of the oppressed, sharing bread with the hungry, and other actions of compassion and mercy (Isa. 58:1–7).

In the legal system, it is assumed that there are classes of disadvantaged people who do not have the means to procure justice for themselves. The poor fall into this category, as do aliens, the needy, all those indicated with the phrase "those who have no helper." In modern terms, these are people who cannot afford a private lawyer. The laws in the Bible exhort the community on behalf of these folk, in order to guarantee for them a measure of equal rights and privileges in court. The taking of bribes and agreeing with the majority or the powerful are to be avoided (Ex. 23:1–9). A witness who aids the guilty for any of these reasons is termed a "violent witness" (Ex. 23:1). That is to say, such a witness commits violence toward those who cannot defend themselves. It is particularly when caught in the net of the legal system that the poor may become aware of the violence that is the mark of their life. Thus, the victim cries out "violence," much like the English "Help!" (Jer. 20:8; Hab. 1:2; Job 19:7).

The psalms especially abound with the pleas of those who feel themselves unjustly accused, against whom violent witnesses testify. In Ps. 27, the believer describes false witnesses as those who breathe out violence (Ps. 27:12). These latter are compared to hunters that set traps or beasts of prey (Ps. 35:7–16).

"They lurk," complains the psalmist, "in secret like a lion in its covert;/they lurk that they may seize the poor;/they seize the poor and drag them off in their net" (Ps. 10:9 NRSV; see also Ps. 57:4–6). The "net" and "the pit" are common imagery in these poems where the "innocent" cry for God to defend them (Ps. 31).

Mockery and insult constitute a common affliction of the poor who cry for help in the psalms. The believer who speaks in Ps. 42 is throughout beset by the taunting of the enemies who say all the day: "Where is your God?" Just so do the enemies of the community mock and deride when it is bowed down and afflicted (Ps. 44, Ps. 74). All the afflicted may call on God and trust in God because they believe that in God's presence is their liberation.

The notion that the poor and the needy demand special attention and that harsh treatment of them is denounced in the strongest language resides in the conviction that the people of the ancient covenant community were to emulate God. God was seen by them as a lover of freedom, an opponent of shackles and burdens, yokes and prisons. Not only did God set the slaves free from Egypt, it was understood that God extended this same zeal to all who are in need of liberating activity. God is the one who gives "food to the hungry." The Maker of heaven and earth is the "maker" of justice for the oppressed (Ps. 146:7–9; see also Deut. 10:12–22).

This understanding of God's nature has profound ramifications for the life of the community that understands itself to be in covenant with God. Christians, together with Jews, are the inheritors of the traditions of ancient Israel. They too understand themselves as a community in covenant with their God. The Christian community views itself, as did ancient Israel, as freed from bondage toward the end of living the life of a redeemed people, an alternative community. The special relationship with God of this alternative community is lived out by emulating the preferences of the God of Israel, by upholding justice for the oppressed in its common life. The human community is called to special responsibility in its modeling itself after a God who abhors the violence of poverty.

The Victims of Violence

Who are the ones especially affected by violence? In the Bible there are certain terms employed for these folk, such as "the poor," "the needy," "those who have no helper," or "the abused." One way to ascertain the identity of groups who are recipients of violence is to identify the victimizer. In respect to the word *hamas*, it is noteworthy that the perpetrators of this type of violence are mostly men. The words "a man of violence" do not find as their counterpart in the Bible "a woman of violence." Men of violence, on the other hand, abound. (See Ps. 18:48; 140:11; Prov. 3:31; 16:29; 2 Sam. 22:49, for example.) Does this mean that men are more prone to violence than women in the view of the biblical writers? I believe that we should rather understand this prevalence of males in connection with violence as an aspect of the structures of patriarchy. Where males are in charge of the structures of family and society, they have the power also to practice violence. Violence then belongs also and foremost to patriarchal structures, and among the victims of violence in these structures, women take a primary place.

A list of folk in the Bible who are in need of special protection are the widow, the orphan, and the stranger. These three comprise women, children, and those who did not belong. Because of their prominence in the laws, in the narratives, and in the prophetic texts, it is clear that in ancient Israel, they were indeed in need of help and that they were automatically victimized by the structures of that ancient society. Again the text stresses that God is on their side and is their protector and helper. Psalm 146, a text already quoted to illustrate God's attention for the poor, specifies this group as the stranger, the orphan, and the widow: "The Lord watches over the strangers;/he upholds the orphan and the widow,/but the way of the wicked he brings to ruin" (Ps. 146:9 NRSV). In Deuteronomy, this watchful support is even more specific when God is said to give them food and clothing (Deut. 10:18). In the laws of Exodus, the direst threats are uttered toward those who abuse the stranger, the widow, and the orphan, whose cries are heard by God. (See Ex. 22:21–24.)

Although the Bible does not offer structures alternative to patriarchy, it condemns consistently the violence that permeates the patriarchal structures and thereby judges these structures themselves to be violent and abusive. The violence extended to women in patriarchy includes poverty but can also take on other forms. The story of Ruth is an extended example of the risk under which widows lived in ancient Israel. Although that story ends well, it was by no means a sure thing, and the narrative is shot through with the fragility and instability of life for single women. Ruth is also a stranger, which exacerbates her situation and makes her doubly prone to violent treatment.

The story of David and Bathsheba is another example of violent treatment of a woman who is made a widow in the course of King David's machinations. This is an interesting example, partly because it is not overtly treated as a rape. The text is clear, however, as to God's displeasure with David's actions (2 Sam. 11:27). When the prophet Nathan tells David his parable, the action is compared to a murder (2 Sam. 12: 1–6). Bathsheba was so violated in the interaction with David that her victimization can be equated with slaughter as Nathan does in the story.

Orphans are basically those without the support of a father. The orphan is identical to the fatherless because basic economic support was lacking without the presence of the father. Fatherless children could be taken away from a widow if a deceased husband had left a debt. The children would then serve the creditor until he judged the debt paid. Such a predicament has overcome the widow who implores Elisha to help her (2 Kings 4:1–4). In that story, Elisha helps the widow to solve not only her immediate problem but to achieve long-term independence for herself and her children.

Strangers were persons without the rights and privileges held by the full members of the community. They lived most vulnerable lives and were in constant need of protection, since they were all potentially marginalized people. Whereas the widow and the orphan were a part of a class of people for whom protection was sought also outside ancient Israel, the concern for the stranger is unique to the Bible. In addition, the laws protecting the stranger are among the most frequently cited and extensive in scope among the law codes of the Hebrew Bible. The community is required to love the stranger (Deut. 10:19 and Lev. 19:34) and to provide for them (Deut. 24:17–22; Lev. 19:9), and is prohibited from oppressing them (Ex. 22:21–23; 23:9). Abuse, exploitation, and oppression toward the stranger are actions that the covenant community must not engage in.

Strangers in the Bible were those who were different from the dominant group. In our society and church, strangers can also be identified in this way. They include people of ethnic minorities, women, persons of different sexual orientation, people with different abilities, the poor; all these are groups that come to mind. Neither the status of the stranger, nor the character of violence, has changed radically. It could even be that the existence of the stranger is more threatened today than it was in the Israel of the past. More than ever, we may need to take to heart the biblical directive to seek the knowledge of the heart of the stranger (Ex. 23:9).

Frequently, in the Bible it is with the stranger or the impoverished woman that liberation is found. When there is drought in the land, Elijah is sent to a widow in Sidon where he finds sustenance and an opportunity to show God's preference for life in spite of her dire situation and deprivation (1 Kings 17:8–24). It is through the widow Ruth that new opportunities for leadership arose in Israel and later through Esther that the community in the dispersion is saved from destruction. Two of these women were also strangers to the covenant community. Jael, who liberated the tribal confederacy from one of its fiercest oppressors, Sisera, was not a member of the tribes herself (Judg. 4:17–22).

To foreswear the violence that is a part of the patriarchal structures, it is necessary to seek new solidarities. In the Bible the prescription for the covenant community is to be on the side of the widow, the orphan, and the stranger, to show allegiance to them. Nothing Jesus said nor did brought any change in these requirements. Rather, Jesus' words underscored their importance. In Jesus' violent death, the evil devisings of the human heart are exposed once more. In breaking the bonds of this death, God once more demonstrated the incapacity of violence to restrain the force of peace. As for us, we must choose where we place ourselves: on the side of violence and death or on the side of peace and life. Fatalism and existence doomed to violence is not a part of biblical thinking. As the biblical text exhorts: "Choose then life, that you may live, you, and your children after you" (Deut. 30:19).

We Won't Let It Happen Here: Keeping Children Safe from Sexual Abuse

Lois Rifner

The director of a childcare program became aware through her work of resources that are available to educate children about child sexual abuse. She also became aware that more and more agencies are screening employees and volunteers for the purpose of reducing the risk of child sexual abuse. She wondered whether her church, with its large church school program and its inhouse day care program, should be concerned. When she raised the question with her pastor, he quickly assured her, "This is a large, well-established church. It can't happen here."

But it does happen here! Child abuse is very much a part of our society, and that includes our churches. An alarming number of children die each year because of child abuse. Many more are physically and emotionally scarred by the trauma of child abuse. National statistics indicate that child abuse is not going away. If one in every three to five children has been sexually victimized in some way before they reach eighteen, some of these children are members of our churches. Some of these victims may confide in their church school teachers or youth group leaders. Some may have even been victimized by church personnel or church volunteers.

One church discovered, to its horror, that many of their preschool children had been sexually molested by two older teens who had volunteered to help with childcare. Although there were adult volunteers in the area, the molestation occurred when individual toddlers were taken to the toilet, which was down the hall. Groups of children were molested when they were taken for walks or scavenger hunts during organized events. When the congregation discovered what was happening, the teens were charged and convicted, and the victims received therapy. But the congregation and the children will never be the same.

Another congregation learned from the media that their beloved youth minister had been arrested for child exploitation that involved youth outside the church. Conflict and tension arose between those in the congregation who believed him innocent and those who thought he should no longer be their youth minister.

Another congregation found that they were the respondent in a lawsuit brought on behalf of children molested by a staff person in the day care housed in their church.

As our society has become more aware of the problem and as regulations have been put in place to protect children from sexual abuse, more and more groups are requiring background checks and affidavits asserting that volunteers have never been reported for, charged with, or found guilty of sexual abuse, exploitation, or other misconduct. As more groups and agencies require such certification, persons who want unsupervised access to children will look for places where this certification is not required. This is one reason why the church must become involved.

Unfortunately, the church is among the last institutions to respond to this crisis. There are a number of reasons for this:

- We are too trusting. We come to church to be spiritually renewed, to feel a part of community. We feel safe in this environment. We find it hard to imagine that some in our spiritual community would betray others.

- We want to think the best of people and to welcome people into our midst. We believe that those who attend church with us will be striving to live Christian lives. We feel that "screening" may give the message that a person is "welcomed," but with certain conditions.

- Our history shows that in many instances we have been too quick to forgive. Perhaps our discomfort with the issue leads us to want to get it behind us so that we can go on with our lives. Perhaps we have concerns about whether the allegations are true and whether we might someday stand accused. Whatever the reason, we have far too often failed to hold those guilty of sexual misconduct accountable—and in so doing we have failed to adequately protect our children.

A number of forces are now causing the church to take a closer look at efforts to prevent child abuse and therefore to accept responsibility as well. Media attention often focuses on child sexual abuse cases, including those cases that involve church workers. The National Child Protection Act of 1993 (see Appendix B on pp. 112–116) urges states to become more insistent on requiring all child-serving agencies and organizations to complete criminal history background checks on all staff and volunteers. Whether this requirement includes churches is not absolutely clear.

Also there are the legal issues. Litigation is on the increase, often resulting in juries awarding astronomical financial settlements. Since many settlements occur out of court, the full extent of financial consequences to insurance companies and/or churches is not known. As this information becomes more available, obtaining criminal background checks and checking personal references of applicants for staff or volunteer positions becomes an area of legal responsibility. If a youngster were to be victimized by a church staff person or volunteer and brought a civil suit against the church as well as the individual, the court would likely find the church negligent if they could have obtained information about the perpetrator and failed to do so. Companies who insure churches are quite aware of this and are increasingly encouraging churches to develop policies for the screening of volunteers and staff.

Reducing the Risk of Child Sexual Abuse in Your Church[1] is a resource package of videos and handbooks developed by Church Law and Tax Report specifically to help with this process. Some insurance companies believe this is so important that they are making this resource available to their insured churches at a greatly reduced cost.

Protecting the church in case of a lawsuit is clearly not the only reason to develop child abuse prevention policies, however. To protect staff and volunteers from the threat of false allegations is also a concern that is increasing with public awareness of child sexual abuse. Without protection, individuals may be much more likely to not want to get involved with children. And if they do get involved, they may be reluctant to provide the hugs and emotional support children need.

---

[1] Richard R. Hammer, Steven W. Klipowicz, and James F. Cobble, Jr., *Reducing the Risk of Child Sexual Abuse in Your Church*, Church Law and Tax Report, 1993. Available from Christian Ministry Resources, P. O. Box 1098, Matthews, NC 28106, 704/841-8066.

In addition to the above reasons, preventing child sexual abuse is also an appropriate mission of the church. The tradition of the Presbyterian Church (U.S.A.) has long been to act in the world wherever injustices are present. This tradition is firmly rooted in the teachings of the Bible and in our Confessions.

The Old Testament is replete with instances of God's blessing on all people, beginning with the creation of the human race in God's image and as the inhabitants of creation that share responsibility with God for the care of creation.

We are reminded in a number of places in the Old Testament to care for orphans and widows, and the orphans are assured that God will hear their cry if they are not treated well. We are encouraged to "train children in the right way," so that "when old, they will not stray" (Prov. 22:6).

We are enjoined by our Confessions and our covenant of baptism to participate in the nurture and guidance of all children of God. Children are to honor their fathers and mothers, but parents are not to provoke their children to anger. The Larger Catechism makes it clear that we are "to love, pray for, and bless [our children]; . . . Protecting, and providing for them all things necessary for soul and body. . . . " (7.239) and that we sin if we "neglect . . . the duties required of [us and by] an inordinate seeking of [our]selves, [our] own glory, ease, profit or pleasure; commanding things unlawful, or not in the power of [children] to perform; counseling, encouraging, or favoring them in that which is evil; dissuading, discouraging, or discountenancing them in that which is good . . . careless exposing or leaving them to wrong, temptation, and danger. . . . " (7.240).

The General Assembly has a long history of promoting that the needs of children be met by our society. Both former denominations and now the reunified Presbyterian Church (U.S.A.) have passed resolutions supporting a reduction in poverty, feeding of the hungry, a reduction in racism, and education for all children. The needs of children, including protection from abuse, were specifically targeted in 1991 and again in 1996.

It is part of God's plan and our response to God's love and grace that each of God's children be nurtured in faith and love. Children cannot grow in faith and know God's love and grace when they are victims of child sexual abuse. The church's complicity or failure to respond to such abuse only compounds the problems experienced by such victims.

Without doubt, what is most important is doing all we can to protect our children, to provide them with an absolutely safe environment in which to learn, grow, share, and journey through their lives.

Our response must not be that "it can't happen here" but rather that *"we won't let it happen here!"*

No Means No:
Acquaintance Rape and Date Rape

Andrea Parrot

Thirty to 40 percent of rapes where the victim and the assailant know one another are outside of a date or romantic setting. These rapes are premeditated, just as stranger rapes are. There is no question of differing expectations or of miscommunication. These rapes are motivated by a need to overpower and humiliate. The rapist isolates the woman and rapes her.

Rape is a violent act of hostility, power, and aggression in which the assailant forces penetration of the vagina, mouth, or anus by the penis or any object against the will and consent of the victim. *Acquaintance rape* is rape by someone the victim knows. *Date rape* is rape by someone the victim has been or is dating.

Even in dating situations, there can be strong elements of the assailant setting up the rape. Often men will date or pick up women who do not appear strong or assertive. They may ply them with alcohol or drugs and/or take them to a secluded place where the sexual assault will occur uninterrupted. Sometimes a man will invite a woman to join him in a group activity in order to allay any initial feelings of discomfort she might have about being out alone with him. Once they are together, the "friends" soon disappear, leaving the assailant and the victim alone.

In many acquaintance rape and most date rape situations, it is sex that the male premeditated, not rape. But when the interaction does not lead to sex as he planned, the male proceeds to take what he feels he deserves—sex. The fact that it is against the woman's will and without her consent makes it rape—whether he uses physical force or not.

Socialization That Is Conducive to a Date Rape Occurrence

Young men and women bring different socializations and peer pressures to relationships. Traditionally, males have been taught to be aggressive, are expected to "score" by their peers, and have been socialized not to take women seriously. Traditionally, females have been taught to put another's feelings and needs before their own, to gauge their worth by their attractiveness to men, and at the same time to guard their reputations as "nice girls." More socially liberal women who don't feel bound by traditional gender roles may be seen as "loose" or "deserving rape" by people viewing them from a conventional gender role standpoint. These differences lead to a myriad of mixed signals and expectations by both men and women in dating and party situations. Coupled with new-found social freedom and experimentation at college, the conditions are particularly conducive to date rape.

Blaming the Victim

In our society, men are expected to initiate sexual activity, women to regulate it. When a rape or attempted rape occurs, the victim is often dismissed as "asking for it" by placing herself in a vulnerable situation and/or not being able to stop the assault. While it is true that a woman may do things that contribute to her vulnerability to becoming victimized, she does not "cause" her rape. The assailant causes the rape by determining that he is going to have sex with her with or without her consent.

Many women fight back; they scream, they struggle, they try to flee. But failing to fight back doesn't cause a rape, as many people mistakenly believe. The victim of date or acquaintance rape may be too drunk or stoned to give consent or to struggle. She may be doing her best to verbally confront him. She may believe that the man will come to his senses at any moment and stop forcing her to have sex. She may be terrified of her attacker and/or his threats. She may fear the consequences of the attention she would draw to the attack if she cried out. She may be so physically overpowered that struggle would accomplish nothing but bring more danger to her. She may be in paralyzing psychological shock.

Her "no" or "stop," however strong or weak, is not heard. Her crying is ignored. But she is making it clear that this is not a mutually desired sexual encounter. It is he who has chosen rape.

Men and women need to communicate honestly early on in their relationship about what they want sexually. Women should learn to trust their instincts, be careful to minimize the factors that make them vulnerable to assault, and assert their expectations clearly. Men need to learn that all interactions with women do not necessarily have to lead to sexual contact. They must also learn that it is never OK to use emotional coercion or physical force on a woman.[1]

---

[1] Taken from "Coping with Date Rape and Acquaintance Rape" and *Acquaintance Rape and Sexual Assault Prevention Training Manual,* by Andrea Parrot. Reprinted with permission from the National Network of Presbyterian College Women. These articles are part of the packet *Young Women Speak: Issues for Study by College Women*, eds. Katie Jacobs and Rebecca Todd Peters, 1994. To order the complete packet, call 1-800-524-2612 and request DMS #72700-94-991. Price $3.50.

Picking Up the Broken Pieces: Responding to Domestic Violence

Marie M. Fortune

As I walked along the Hawaiian beach on a vacation evening, I noticed many bits of glass of all colors—green, brown, clear—some smoothed by the incessant pounding of the waves, others still sharp and ominous. I began to pick them up for a couple of reasons: I didn't want to step on them, and I didn't want anyone else to either. By the time I had returned to my cottage, I had a handful of glass.

The next morning, I walked again, and again the bits of glass were spread over the beach. Again I gathered them up as I went and returned with a handful. Evening and morning I repeated this ritual. I would clean the beach of glass, and on my next walk after the tide had come and gone, I would find still more glass. The supply of broken glass seemed limitless.

I wondered where the glass was coming from and why it was broken to begin with. In addition to this reflection on the root causes of the problem, the fact was that it was useful to pick up fragments of glass each day, if only to prevent the next person from cutting her feet.

There are many days when this experience is a metaphor for my ministry. Day in and day out, from our beaches we retrieve the pieces of our brokenness caused by violence and try to prevent the next person from being harmed—only to realize that the bigger question must be contemplated out there in the ocean of our shared lives.

Here I will address domestic violence, offer new insights perhaps, assess our progress as religious people responding to this problem, and suggest some of the challenges ahead of us.

Domestic violence is the shorthand term commonly used to describe the abuse of one adult partner by the other in an intimate relationship. Ann Jones in her latest book, *Next Time, She'll Be Dead*, points out that domestic violence is a euphemistic term. Domestic violence describes the geographic location of the abuse but tells us nothing about the who and what. Although domestic violence can occur in heterosexual, gay, or lesbian relationships, and although men can on occasion be victims of women partners, the vast majority of domestic violence involves men abusing women.

Why must we address violence against women? Why not violence against persons? I am concerned about violence against persons, whether it is gang violence or political violence or crime in the streets violence. But in a patriarchal society, if we are to understand the particulars of personal violence, we must use a gender analysis. Using the lens of gender will reveal some very important aspects for us. Statistics paint the outline of the picture:

- One in five women is raped in her lifetime.
- African-American women are almost twice as likely to be raped as white women.
- 78 percent of rapes are committed by relatives, friends, or neighbors.
- Women in the United States are more likely to be assaulted and injured, raped, or killed by a current or former partner than by acquaintances, other family members, and strangers combined.

- Each year 30 percent of the women who are murdered are killed by husbands, boyfriends, or former partners.
- For every serial killer like Jeffery Dahmer who preys on young men and boys, there are nine serial killers murdering women.
- Since 1974, the rates for assault and other crimes against women have increased dramatically, but the rates for the same crimes against men have declined.
- The average prison sentence of men who kill their woman partners is two to six years.
- Women who kill their partners are sentenced on average to fifteen years, despite the fact that most women who kill do so in self-defense.
- 64 percent of women in a survey of 20,000 military personnel reported sexual harassment.
- 35 to 40 percent of battered women attempt suicide.
- Wife abuse accounts for 25 percent of suicides by all U.S. women and 50 percent of suicides by African-American women.

Physical and sexual violence against women, usually committed by men, is endemic in our culture. The high rates of violence against women and girl children make it clear that we who are female are particularly vulnerable to violence simply due to our gender. This is a fact of life that we women know in our heads and hearts. We live with the reality that theologian Mary Hunt has described as violence being the context *of* our lives rather than separate, individual episodes *in* our lives. It is the broken glass on the beaches we walk every day.

There is one significant difference between women's and men's experiences of violence. For men, personal violence is episodic. It occurs occasionally to individuals. It occurs more frequently to men who, by virtue of their occupation, are at great risk, e.g., in the military, professional sports, drug dealing, or police work. Their occupation may require them to be in harm's way.

But as women, we live in harm's way. Every day, everywhere. There is no respite. And we are statistically more at risk at home than in public. Physical and sexual violence is the context of our lives. We get up in the morning and go to work or to school in spite of this knowledge. In other words, we use denial to help us cope with the reality around us. The knowledge of our vulnerability dramatically shapes our lives. It affects our decisions about what job to take, what hours to work, what school to attend, what movies to see, whom we spend time with, how we relate to our families, whether and where to jog, hike, or walk.

We must recognize that violence against women is a social problem, not merely an individual one. It is a reality that is congruent with the patriarchal culture and values of our society. And so it is important to address it in its particularity. At the same time, we must remember that violence and the threat of violence are common experiences in women's individual lives.

This is nothing new. Recall the story in Judges 19 of the unnamed concubine who is eventually sacrificed to a gang of men determined to assault her master. She is raped, beaten, and left for dead. There are other equally vivid stories of violence against women within our biblical tradition and our collective history.

Consider your own lives. How many of you know a neighbor, family member, or friend—or you yourself—who has experienced rape, incest, sexual abuse, battering, harassment? Violence in women's lives is a common thread that weaves our experiences together. And if we are honest, we will recognize that these common experiences among us are common experiences among members of our congregations as well.

Pastors are very well aware of this because your people have shared their experiences with you. Some of you can relate to this description of the local church that comes from a United Church of Canada pastor. After describing the multiple cases of abuse to which she has attempted a pastoral response, she has concluded: "I look out my window at the blue sky and the green leaves, the traffic and the pedestrians, and it hardly seems possible that there's a war on. But I really believe there is, and this quiet little church is a MASH unit."

It is absolutely appropriate that this issue of violence against women be before us for at least two reasons.

The first is pastoral. Our people are hurting. Families and individuals are being destroyed by violence. Children are growing up believing that daddy hitting mommy is just the way things are. Many women live with the fact that their home is the most dangerous place for them to be. People need to know that they can come to their church for support and information and, when they come, they need to find church leaders prepared to assist them.

The second is pragmatic. The issue of violence against women needs to be one of the priorities of a peacemaking agenda because it is a social issue that is personal and immediate in our lives right here. The fact that women and girls in our culture learn early that we have no right to bodily integrity, that we have no right to be free from bodily harm, is a fact that has long been accepted as normal.

The church in its silence has been and continues in many ways to be complicit in this reality for women and is often the source of justification. We've been good on other violence issues: capital punishment, nuclear proliferation, gang violence, nonviolence as political strategy, and so on. Until fifteen years ago there was virtually nothing in theology, biblical studies, pastoral care, and ethics that mentioned rape, battering, incest, or other forms of sexual and domestic violence.

What is this violence?

- It is physical violence: punching, kicking, slapping, throwing objects, using weapons (knives, bats, cars, acid).
- It is sexual violence: forced sexual activity, often following a beating.
- It is psychological violence: not unlike brainwashing, similar to what hostages experience.
- It is psychological coercion backed by the threat of violence.
- It is the destruction of property and pets: always the object or pet that belongs to the victim so the message is clear, "This time it is the dog; next time it is you."

I use the term "violence" conservatively. By violence I mean the use of physical force or the threat of physical force to control another person. Violence describes the behavior. How we evaluate the behavior depends on a number of factors. On some occasions, violence may be justified. One example is the use of physical force to protect oneself or another from harm, which may well be justified and necessary. Generally speaking, the use of physical force to control a family member, friend, or employee is never justified.

If you want to understand the dynamics of personal violence within its institutional context, consider the film *Schindler's List*. The commandant of the camp where the Jews were held was a batterer. He had power over the Jews, and he used violence and the threat of violence to control their behavior, whether the Jews in the camp or in his household. His violence was arbitrary, usually well-thought-out, intentional, not the result of his loss of temper. It worked very well to keep the camp under his control. He used violence with impunity.

Schindler, in an effort to lessen the abuse of the Jews, suggested that the commandant could in fact exercise more control by using less violence. The thought of more control attracted the commandant. And he instituted Schindler's suggestion. This tactic worked because everyone knew that at any moment he could kill them. The threat of violence replaced the acts of violence and served his purpose well. The commandant used violence as a means to an end—and he did so because he could. He was not accountable to anyone for his means, only for his ends. The pattern he portrayed in the film is played out every day in families across the United States.

So much for the who and the what. What are we doing about it? Have we made progress in addressing this reality in the past twenty years? Yes and no. The issues are before us everyday in the media, and some education has been accomplished through this attention. The eventual response to the murder of Nicole Brown Simpson is a case in point. Finally, the media have made a connection between the history of O. J. Simpson's battering of his wife (which is public record) and the possibility that he murdered her. Hence, there has been an intensive investigative reporting on battered women. The church can no longer deny the reality of sexual and physical abuse. In some instances, the church has even been able to name and confess its complicity in the abuse of women. The Catholic Bishops of Canada have stated that the church must take responsibility for the abuse of women when it has directed abused women to remain in relationships with batterers and when it has taught women's subordination in marriage. Perhaps we are beginning to understand that the church is a part of the problem, that the church has contributed mightily to the context that has long tolerated the abuse of women.

In the United States, there is legislation that specifically addresses violence against women. The Surgeon General has named domestic violence as a public health issue. The American Medical Association has also acknowledged that domestic violence is the number one threat to women's health.

There are basic services that assist battered women in many communities, but they are never adequate. In Philadelphia, 75 percent of battered women who seek shelter are turned away. Rape crisis centers and women's shelters are still not understood as necessary services along with police and fire departments.

Unfortunately, legal decisions to support battered women and rape victims are being reversed. State laws requiring arrest of batterers are not being enforced. At the same time, battered women who kill their batterers are still being convicted and given long sentences.

Why so little progress? There has been no fundamental change of belief. We still do not believe that women have the right to be free from bodily harm. We still do not believe that men who abuse women must be held accountable. We can build more shelters, pass more laws, train more people, establish more advocacy programs, build more prisons; but if we don't have individual police officers, judges, doctors, clergy, friends, therapists who believe that every woman has the right to be free from bodily harm and that men who abuse women must be held accountable, then our systemic responses will be for naught.

Tracey Thurman's story is a case in point: it is fairly well known because she brought a successful lawsuit against the police department that didn't protect her. She had left her abusive husband and taken her child. He refused a divorce. He continually harassed her, repeatedly threatening to kill her. She had a restraining order, but when she called the police, they said they couldn't do anything because it was a holiday weekend. Every time he came to her home and threatened her, she would call and the police would not respond.

The last time, an officer drove up and sat in the car while her husband chased her across the yard, grabbed her by the hair, slashed her face with a knife, knocked her down and stabbed her twelve times. The officer finally approached the batterer, who gave him the knife, but the officer made no arrest. The officer then stood by and watched as the batterer kicked Tracey and broke her neck. As they were putting her into the ambulance, her husband attacked her again. Finally he was restrained by the officers. Thurman survived, disfigured and partially paralyzed. Her husband was convicted of assault and sentenced to prison.

Consider the O. J. Simpson case. We know that Simpson battered his wife. The legal system supposedly intervened and required community service and counseling. When he didn't have time for either, the community service sentence was suspended and the therapy was carried out by a psychiatrist over the phone. Anna Quindlen of the *New York Times* raised the question: "If Simpson had pleaded no contest to drug charges instead of wife abuse, would Hertz and NBC have continued to employ him? I think not" (*Seattle Times*, June 22, 1994).

We do not believe that women have the right to be free of bodily harm and that men who abuse women should be held accountable.

A subtext to lack of male accountability is the lengths to which some batterers will go to find their partners. Not only are they not accountable, they have no shame. It is becoming a common practice for batterers to hire private investigators to find the women whose lives they have threatened and who have gone to great lengths to hide from them. One woman called the police, got a protection order, fled to a shelter, and used the state address confidentiality program to remove her address from documents. Not long after, she found her abusive husband on her doorstep. He had hired a private investigator. Although terrified, she gave up and let him move back in because she decided there was no way to hide. Some investigators don't take cases involving a batterer tracking his partner, but others do. For only $150, a batterer can usually find the woman who is running from him.

Consider the comments made by men from the United States, Australia, and Europe, who travel to Asia, particularly Thailand, on sex tours. The advertisements entice men with anonymity and nonaccountability: "Go where no one will know you or care what you do." They do, and they don't deny this advantage. They say, "I can do things here I can't do at home; and I'm looking for women who will do what they are told, not like United States women who are getting too uppity."

Sometimes people—especially church people—get uncomfortable when we talk about accountability. They want to begin with forgiveness, mercy, and grace. But this is bad theology and worse exegesis. In Luke's Gospel: "If your brother offends against you, rebuke him; and if he repents, forgive him" (Luke 17:3). There is a whole lot that precedes forgiveness here, for the offender's sake and for ours.

I was meeting with a group of incest offenders who were in a court-mandated treatment program. I had been asked to discuss religious issues with them because out of the twenty-seven men, twenty-five were Christians, and they had a lot of questions. At the end of the evening, they made this request of me: "Whenever you talk with church people, tell them not to forgive us so quickly." Each of them had gone directly to their pastor after their arrest for molesting their children. Each had been prayed over and sent home "forgiven." They said it was the worst thing anyone could have done to them because it allowed them to continue to avoid responsibility for the harm they had done. Their witness is a powerful challenge to us all.

Accountability is the way to stop the abuse of women—and we have much to learn about accountability. I was speaking in southeastern Alaska a number of years ago and was in dialogue with members of the Tlingit tribe, who reflected on their history. They have a memory of a time a hundred years ago when, in their tribe, wife abuse was forbidden. The community norm was clear: you didn't beat your wife. If you violated the norm, there was a predictable response. Your family had to make material restitution to your wife's family in a public gathering. Consequently, there was rarely an incident of wife abuse. It was shameful and expensive.

A hundred years later, after the arrival of white settlers and alcohol, those community norms have been badly damaged; their incidence of wife abuse and alcoholism equals that of the rest of the United States. But the advantage the Tlingit people have is a memory of a time when the norm of their community supported safety for women. They are now seeking to recover that norm.

This illustrates the theological and ethical mandates for justice making that, for us as a faithful people who claim to be rooted in the Hebrew and Christian traditions, should be fundamental to our commitment and actions. We may not have the specificity of the Tlingit tradition, but we have a clear mandate within biblical tradition:

- The powerful words of the Hebrew prophets that call those who harm others to repent, that name the truth of violence and abuse.
- The words of longing for justice in the midst of deeds of violence.
- God's promise in Isaiah 58:8–9.
- The Gospel story of the good Samaritan who stops to aid the victim of violence and take that person to a safe place.
- The example of the persistent widow who goes back again and again to the unjust judge, demanding justice for herself and her cause.
- Jesus' anger at those who would defile the sacred, and his unequivocal call to repentance for those who have harmed others.

All of these teachings point us to justice making. In 1869, John Stuart Mill, referring to equal rights for women, wrote: "If the principle is true, we ought to act as if we believe it."

If we believe that women have the right to be free from bodily harm and that those who abuse them should be held accountable, then we ought to act as if we believed it.

I know that many do act as if you believe it. I applaud and appreciate those who in your worklife are providing services to women and their children who are victims of violence; those of you who serve on boards for agencies, who raise money, who give money, who teach about these issues in our colleges and seminaries; those of you who have found a way out of an abusive situation for yourself and your children; those of you who are pastors, therapists, judges, friends who are holding abusers and incest offenders accountable; those of you who serve as advocates for battered women and rape victims; those of you who seek to change the laws that have for so long not attended to women's experiences.

I applaud all of you who are keeping the faith. You are picking up the broken glass off the beaches; you are helping to piece some of the glass back together; and you are working to insure that fewer glasses, vases, bottles, vessels of the human spirit get broken.

I challenge you to continue your efforts or to take on new tasks in your churches and communities:

- Adopt a shelter or rape crisis center as a mission project.
- Offer meeting space for victims of abuse to meet.
- Help raise money.
- Lobby the legislature.
- Raise money for scholarships for formerly battered women.
- Write letters to the editor when the press refuse to call the murder-suicide committed by a husband domestic violence.
- Do Bible study about women's stories of abuse and of courage in Scripture.

How do we all sustain ourselves in these efforts? I go to baseball games and remind myself that batting .300 is good, that pitching a complete game is no small feat, that tomorrow is another game, and that some days are, as Yogi Berra said, "just déjà vu all over again." I also pray. I am sustained by the witness of courage and hope that I experience from women who resist men's violence, who have gotten away, who have managed to piece their lives back together. They embody the kind of persistent hope that Václav Havel, the president of the Czech Republic, describes: "Hope isn't about believing that we can change things. Hope is about believing that what we do matters." And I cherish my anger. I know that when I stop being angry about what I hear and read and see every day, I will have given up hope and I will no longer have the capacity for compassion or action.

Finally, I try to act as if I believe what I learned in church. That's all I can ask of myself or of you. That is all that God asks of us.

This article is reprinted by permission of Church and Society, vol. 85 no. 3 (January/February 1995), pp. 36–47.

Ageing and Ageism: Implications for the Church's Ministry with Families

Thomas B. Robb

Some people have always lived to be very old, but not until the twentieth century have the majority of entire populations lived to advanced age. This phenomenon has had profound impact on nearly every social institution. The church has not been exempt.

Since the beginning of this century, the number of Americans over age 65 has grown from 3 million, 4 percent of the population, to 30 million, more than 12 percent. Average life expectancy has risen from 47 years to 78 years. This change, unlike anything in recorded history, is the result of a dramatic drop in the death of infants and children. Improved sanitation, better access to health care, and the elimination and control of infectious diseases have increased the probability of long life. As a result:

- The number of adults age 65 and older now exceeds the number of teenagers in the United States.
- The number of adults age 50 and older now exceeds the total number of elementary and high school students in the U.S.
- One-fourth of the members of the Presbyterian Church (U.S.A.) are over age 65, and one half are over age 50.

Add improvements in Social Security, as well as generous public and private retirement income programs, and the economic results are equally dramatic:

- The incidence of poverty among white males over age 65 is lower than the rest of the population, and much lower than the rate among children.
- Adults age 50 and older now have more disposable income than teenagers and young urban professionals combined.
- Adults age 50 and older control more than three-fourths of all the assets in the United States.
- Three-fourths of those over age 65 own the homes they live in, and four out of five elderly homeowners have paid off the mortgages on their homes.

Older adults don't share equally in these blessings, however. Many find their later years anything but golden:

- Age, race, marital status, and length of time retired all adversely affect economic being in retirement.
- Older white women, and both older men and older women among most minority groups, have a poverty rate much higher than that of children.
- The suicide rate for people over 65, 18.5 per 100,000, is 50 percent higher than the rest of the population, 12 per 100,000. The rate is 24.1 for those aged 75–84, and 19.1 for those over age 85.

Over the next forty years, we can expect still more dramatic changes:

- Average life expectancy at birth, now 78 years, will rise to more than 90 years.

- The median age of the U.S. population, now 33 years, will increase to more than 40 years.

- When the baby-boom generation retires, the age group 65 and over, now 12.5 percent, will increase to more than 21 percent of the total population.

- The age group 19 to 64 will increase in numbers but remain constant as a percentage of the total population. The age group 18 and younger will remain constant in numbers but decrease as a percentage of the total.

- The fertility rate (the average number of children a woman bears during her lifetime), now 1.8, will remain below the replacement rate (the number of births per woman required for a generation to replace itself), 2.1, as it has for nearly three decades.

- The birth rate, the total number of children born during a given time period, will drop sharply as the baby-boom generation completes middle age and their children, the "echo" generation, complete their childbearing years.

These changing patterns are not confined to the United States. Every modern, technological nation is experiencing similar changes. Over the next forty to sixty years, nearly all third-world nations are expected to experience changes of the same magnitude but at an even faster rate.

Such dramatic population shifts have a significant impact on social institutions. When births increase, schools, colleges, and the job market must expand to make room for them. When births decline, these same institutions must downsize. When change is large-scale and rapid, both expansion and downsizing can jeopardize their stability.

During the population explosion of the 1950s and early 1960s, churches were organized, built, and enlarged to match the rapid growth of the suburbs. As those suburbs and their residents have aged, congregations that once numbered 500 to 1,000 members have shrunk to 200–300.

At least two factors will impact the future of most churches:

- The average age of the congregation's membership will continue to rise as the birth rate drops, the fertility rate remains low, and longevity rises because of further improvements in health care.

- Every effort to increase the number of children and youth in church school and youth programs will be limited by low fertility and birth rates.

Ageism: Feelings beyond Facts

Ageism is the attribution of undesirable characteristics to an individual or a group solely on the basis of age. It is the root of a great deal of prejudice, discrimination, and abuse. It has been around for a very long time, and it may be on the rise in our land.

Moses' injunction, "Honor your father and your mother, so that your days may be long in the land" (Ex. 20:12), may reveal that the elderly were neglected or abused during the wilderness years, and that such was still the case centuries later when the Torah was reduced to writing. Such an admonition would hardly be necessary if respect and dignity were the norm.

The accusation that Israel's leaders made unjust laws so they could seize the property of widows (Isa. 10:1–2), the appointment of deacons to distribute food to widows (Acts 6:1–6), and the assertion that genuine religion includes the care of widows (James 1:27), suggests that ageism, at least toward women, continued to be a problem in Israel.

The origins of contemporary ageism lie, in part, in the beginnings of the very social services upon which many older people now rely. Organizations formed to aid the poor focused their efforts on those whose lot was deemed most likely to improve. The old were then systematically excluded on the ground that their characters were past reforming and they had outlived the years of productivity.[1]

Some charitable organizations did establish homes to provide the indigent elderly with the bare essentials of food and shelter. In the process, they laid the groundwork for the segregation of older people into residences apart from the rest of society. The subsequent development of nursing homes, senior centers, and retirement villages perpetuates the notion that the old are to be cared for away from the rest of us, and that they prefer it so.

The growth of the study of gerontology, together with the development of a wide range of social services for the elderly, has contributed to the spread of ageism. Scholars and advocates have so unremittingly described the unfortunate situation of many older people that they have convinced us that all those over age 65 are sickly, poor, forgetful, unable to have or enjoy sex, and vulnerable to sharp con men.

Even those who try to be helpful are often unwittingly guilty of ageism. Some years ago, National Parks superintendents were brought together to learn how to make their facilities more accessible to those with limiting impairments. Aging was listed as an area of concern, along with visual, hearing, learning, and mobility impairments. While many older people experience such limitations, age is not itself a handicap—except when others make it so.

The Social Security Act has done more than other institutions in American society to prevent widespread poverty and indigence among the old. However, by establishing age 65 as a formidable barrier between the generations, it too has done its share in spreading ageism.

Backlashes and Responses

When a group long subjected to prejudice and discrimination begins to assert its claim to the rights enjoyed by the majority, a backlash often results. Violence against Blacks increased markedly during the bus boycotts, lunch-counter sit-ins, voter registration drives, and students' attempts to enroll in white high schools and universities. Women often find career advancement stymied by a "glass ceiling" that prevents promotion to top positions. Others find themselves subjected to sexual harassment. Gays and lesbians who revealed their sexual orientation have lost their jobs and been dismissed from the military. Others have been beaten and some have been killed.

A similar backlash seems to be developing toward older people as their numbers increase and the cost of Social Security, Medicare, and other entitlements rises rapidly. Expressions like "greedy geezers" and "woopies" (well-off older people) have come into widespread use. Older people have been blamed for budget deficits, increases in the national debt, and other economic woes.

Recently, efforts have been made to create the impression that older people are no longer worse off than others. This has been used as a rationale for cutting back on services and entitlements for the old. Groups like the Association for Generational Equity have promoted equal treatment for all ages—which in effect seems to mean cutting back on older people's services and entitlements.

It is argued that children, as a group, are poor far more often than older people. It is reasoned that, since they have many more years of productivity ahead of them, resources should be diverted from the elderly to programs of benefit to children. Organizations once devoted solely to the concerns of the elderly have taken up this theme, perhaps in self-defense.

Ageism often takes the form of discrimination in the workplace. Ample evidence is available that older workers are more productive, more creative, more loyal, and less likely to be absent than younger workers, yet employers continue to choose younger applicants. Older applicants are told they are over qualified or that they cannot qualify for medical insurance or pension plans. Older employees are passed over for promotions, receive smaller pay increases, and are often the first to be let go when companies are scaled back. Sometimes older workers are let go just before becoming eligible for company retirement plans.

Under the federal Age Discrimination in Employment Act and the Employee Retirement Income Security Act, all such practices are illegal. Many workers do not know their rights, and few claims are filed for redress of such abuses.

The Older Americans Act establishes adequate income, good health, suitable housing, employment for those who want to work, and pursuit of meaningful activity as criteria for the quality of older people's life. Other federal statutes, notably the Age Discrimination Act, require that older adults receive their fair share of public spending for housing, social services, transportation, and the like. When budget cuts must be made, programs for the elderly often face dismantling or defunding. Often the arguments promote the idea that younger people have a future, older people don't; younger people will be productive, older people can't.

And the Churches?

Churches and their leaders, too, are often guilty of ageism. "Youth are the future of the church" is often the rallying cry of those engaged in planning, budgeting, or seeking a new pastor. A congregation composed largely of middle-aged and retired people will tell a prospective pastor they want someone to "get their youth back" even when there are now few youth in the surrounding community. A similarly graying congregation with few constituents under age 18 will often budget heavily for church and youth programs and provide little or nothing for ministries with older people.

Many congregations weight their programs heavily toward families with children and neglect the needs of single young adults and older people whose children are grown or who never had children. When questioned, leaders reply that everything they offer is open to all adults, and of course older people are welcome.

The concerns and needs of older adults are often quite different from those of young families. Once their children are grown and educated, those in later middle age often embark on new ventures or undertake to deepen their spiritual resources. Those who have retired often look for ways to use skills and experience in new ways, especially through organizations that help people.

If what the church offers them is planned around the needs of younger families, it will miss their interests and fail to provide them with opportunities for continued growth and development. If what is offered is not planned with any group's needs in mind, it will miss almost everyone's concerns.

Among the most pervasive forms of ageism present in many congregations are the assumptions that people get more religious as they grow older, that older people prefer things as they have been and will resist anything new, and that older adults prefer the company of other older adults and do not want children around. All are far from the truth. Age has nothing to do with such differences. We all tend to continue the religious practices we learned earlier in life. Some are always ready to try something new, others aren't. Some people enjoy children, some don't.

Getting in the church and getting to the church are two areas where ageism often operates. Steps at every entrance, events scheduled on an upper floor, and restrooms and toilet stalls too small for a wheelchair can be a barrier for those who have difficulty climbing stairs or must use a walker or wheelchair. Such barriers have a way of saying, "You're not welcome here." Members who live in a nursing home, need help getting dressed, use a walker or wheelchair, find it hard to drive at night, or have given up their cars will likely have difficulty getting to worship and other church events. They may be reluctant to ask for a ride and just stay home instead. A lack of sensitivity to their situation can translate into, "We've forgotten you."

An Opportunity for Ministry

Ministry with older adults is seldom seen as an essential part of a congregation's ongoing program. The denominational retirement home is expected to meet the most pressing needs. It is assumed that Sunday worship, adult church school classes, and women's and men's programs, together with the community senior center and congregate meal site, meet most other needs. There is often little awareness of needs and concerns particular to this time of life. Challenges to spiritual growth and discipleship are seldom offered.

The demographics of our existence have changed. No longer are we a nation with large numbers of children and relatively fewer numbers at each later stage of life. We are rapidly approaching the time when nearly everyone will live into their 80s and 90s and the numbers in each of the first seven decades of life will be roughly the same. Our commitments to affirmative action and equal employment opportunity include a commitment to fair treatment of older workers. Surely the same ought to be true of our dealings with older church members.

If further incentive is needed, a quick review of members' giving should prove enlightening. Older people often have far more disposable income than younger families, and in many congregations half to three-fourths of the budget is funded by retired members. It is not unduly crass to ask whether they are getting a fair return on their investment in the Kingdom.

Our understandings about the nature of life have changed, too. No longer are our years neatly divided into successive stages of education, work, and leisure. Leisure is seen as important at every age, education has become lifelong, and many choose to find work well into the years set aside for retirement and leisure. The church needs to provide opportunity for older adults to resume the spiritual growth they put on hold while raising their children, and to explore new forms of discipleship as careers wind down.

Transitional rites—baptism, confirmation, marriage, and even the funeral—help the individual and the congregation understand and celebrate events that move us forward into a new stage of life. They tell us how to behave and instruct others how to treat us and what to expect of us. Similar rites are needed to mark the now-common transitions of the empty nest, when the last child leaves the household; retirement, when work ceases; and that point where infirmity and dependence on others become the norm.

Discretionary time increases once the children are grown, and again following retirement. Opportunities abound for travel and leisure pursuits. Fearing they won't have enough to do, some folks plunge into such activities without probing whether that's what they most want to do with their lives. This is a good time to invite church members to explore at some depth what God has in mind for them now.

Everyone needs to smell the roses, and those who haven't taken time earlier may have some catching up to do when they first retire. Others ought to be allowed some time just to sit and rock. We should not be hesitant, however, about challenging older people with new opportunities for service and leadership. Most do not want to be put on the shelf. They want to continue to use their experience and skills and to do things they have never done before.

The Gift of a Lifetime Project, part of the Presbyterian Church (U.S.A.) from 1985 to 1989,[2] asked retired Presbyterians to give two years' full-time volunteer service to development of older adult ministries in churches around the country. Several participants said this was the first time since they had retired that the church had asked them to do anything meaningful. From Wasatch Academy to the mountains of Nepal, older Presbyterians have served as Volunteers in Mission, often in circumstances far from comfortable and usually at their own expense. Similarly, the Peace Corps has expanded opportunities in order to meet the demand from older people for appointments overseas.

Older people are hungry for learning opportunities, too. Every year, hundreds of thousands register for Elderhostel courses all over the world. Middle-aged and older adults are enrolling in colleges and seminaries in record numbers. Lay schools of theology draw large numbers of older people to in-depth courses in Bible, theology, church history, missions, and the like. In every congregation there are retired teachers and professors, and others who have always wanted to teach but never had an opportunity.

Caring for the Elderly

In every congregation there are families caring for aging relatives. Caring for the elderly is largely a family affair: as many disabled older people are cared for by families at home as are cared for in nursing homes. If we add help with personal and household activities, three times as many are cared for at home as in nursing homes. The widespread belief that families callously dump older relatives into nursing homes is largely a myth. Most families take that step only long after financial and emotional resources and individual strength have been exhausted.

The stresses of caregiving often lead to family violence. There is anger toward the parent whose needs consume money, time, and energy. Incontinence, memory lapses, and the changes wrought by strokes and Alzheimer's disease evoke impatience. Hurt feelings left over from childhood sometimes resurface. Spouses and children become frustrated when their needs and wants are neglected or deferred. Anger and frustration turn to physical and emotional violence. Sometimes it is aimed at the older family member, sometimes it is displaced onto spouse or children.

Family caregivers need support and they need relief from time to time. Churches can provide support groups that afford caregivers opportunity to compare notes with others, support each other, express their frustration and anger in a safe environment, and learn about community resources that can help them. Churches can also provide respite, chiefly in the form of a volunteer who moves in and cares for the older person while family members go out to dinner, take in a movie, or get away for a weekend or a short vacation.

Finally, pastors and volunteers can provide personal support and counsel to help families cope with the stresses of caregiving and work through decisions about when to turn caregiving over to professionals.

The Reality of Frustration

In every congregation there are also older people whose desire to make the most of life is frustrated by illness, reduced income, physical or mental impairment, or limited education. Some live alone or with relatives, others live in nursing homes and retirement housing. Some need help coping with routine activities of daily life, some need transportation, some just need information. In every community there are agencies whose purpose is to help them overcome these limitations.

Too often older people don't know what help is available or where or how to get it. One older man pushed his walker several miles to get food stamps because he didn't know that free van transportation was available. Churches need to gather information about where basic services are provided and be prepared to make referrals. Sometimes they may also need to provide a ride or go with an older person and help them communicate or fill out forms.

There is no need for churches to duplicate services already available in the community. They can support those agencies by providing space for their activities, making their kitchens available to meals-on-wheels programs, providing volunteers to deliver meals or help staff programs, opening their fellowship halls for congregate meals, circulating information to older people about their programs, and providing resources in the form of money and equipment.

Death and Ministry

Two of the most common experiences of later life are the terminal illness, and the death, of a spouse. In other times, death might come at any age, and often came swiftly as the result of infectious disease or a serious accident. Now death comes most often in later life, and usually as the final, drawn-out stage of chronic illness or debilitating disease. Pastoral care and counsel during such times is a ministry for which the church is uniquely suited because the church, unlike the rest of the community, understands that death is part of life and the challenge is to deal with it well.

Medical technology has provided us with machines that can prolong some aspects of life long after death would otherwise have occurred. Spouses and family members must often make difficult decisions about whether such devices should be used, and sometimes about whether they should be turned off. Support groups can enable those who have dealt with such decisions to support and counsel those now facing them. Such groups also afford a safe environment for dealing with feelings of frustration and anger that are common at such times.

One member of almost every married couple will experience the death of the other. The loss of a spouse after many years can bring deep feelings of loss, anger, disorientation, frustration, and despair. Few are prepared for such loss, even when it is preceded by a long illness. Most will need support while they figure out how life will go on. Again, support groups are an appropriate way to bring together those recently widowed and those who have survived the experience.

The end of a marriage through divorce, although less common than the death of one spouse, can be equally devastating. Because many of the feelings are the same and just as intense, it can be feasible to include divorced individuals in a support group for the recently widowed.

The Challenge of Retirement

Retirement, or the retirement of one's spouse, can also be unsettling, even when planned well in advance. Few of us are fully prepared for the loss of structure and associations when we depart the workplace. The feelings we experience are similar to those associated with other major losses. Support groups are once again an appropriate tool for helping individuals adjust to retirement. Study groups in advance of retirement are also practical. In both cases, opportunity should be provided for considering the meaning and purpose of life and exploring what opportunities retirement may afford for deepened faith and spiritual meaning and for new forms of service and discipleship.

Churches are a natural environment for support groups. Some pastors are well-suited to serve as facilitators of such groups. Outside leadership can be secured through community mental health centers and sometimes through neighborhood senior centers.

Conclusion

Support for the basic rights of today's elderly is, after all, a matter of self-interest. The way our society treats older people now is likely the way it will treat us in a few years—or, for some, the way it is treating us now. The prevalence of ageism and discrimination against the old would therefore seem to call for advocacy similar to past activities of churches on behalf of minorities and women. Churches contemplating corporate advocacy should first learn about the limitations on lobbying that, if violated, can jeopardize their tax-exempt status. Individual church members, of course, are free to support particular legislation and candidates.

The prospect of one's own later years, and the accompanying fear of declining health and increasing dependence on others, may invest ageing with a dynamic of fear that leads to ageism. This seems analogous to the way, as some have suggested, that fear of our own tendency toward violence leads to demands for tougher law enforcement, and fear of latent homosexuality in ourselves leads to homophobia and even violence toward gays and lesbians.

It may be, therefore, that empowering older people is a more promising activity for congregations. Most of the activities described here—opportunities for service, learning opportunities, help in coping with impairments, support groups for those in crisis or transition— can help older people retain or recover control over their lives.

Notes

1. Carole Haber, *Beyond Sixty-Five* (New York: Cambridge University Press, 1983), pp. 37–39.

2. Three manuals were developed during the Gift of a Lifetime Project and are available from the Presbyterian Distribution Service (1-800–524–2612):

- *Older Adult Ministry: Resource for Program Development* (#21785429)
- *Older Adult Ministry: Guide for Presbytery Committee* (#18090300)
- *Older Adult Ministry: A Guide for the Session and Congregation* (#18090301)

This article is reprinted by permission of Church and Society, *vol. 84 no. 2 (November/December 1993), pp. 109–121.*

Part 2

Suggested Workshops

O LORD, you will hear the desire of the meek;
  you will strengthen their heart,
    you will incline your ear
to do justice for the orphan and the oppressed,
  so that those from earth may strike terror no more.
                                    —*Psalm 10:17–18*

The following exercise, "What Is Domestic Violence Anyway?" will help participants further their own understanding of the complexities involved in addressing domestic violence. It is recommended that this exercise be done before focusing on child abuse, acquaintance rape and date rape, spouse abuse, and elder abuse in order to establish a foundation within the group for what domestic violence is and is not.

What Is Domestic Violence Anyway?

1. Read the following aloud to the group:

Domestic violence is manifested in many ways. It can be overt, as in cases of physical violence, where often times the abuse is apparent in bruises and broken bones. It can also be subtle and much more difficult to describe, which is often the case in sexual, emotional, or psychological violence. There are also times when culturally accepted norms for discipline can be abusive. Regardless of the nature of the violence, it has devastating effects on the functioning of a family and the individuals involved.

2. Distribute a copy of the "Domestic Violence Worksheet" found on page 32 to each participant.

3. After each participant has had an opportunity to fill out the sheet, ask the members of the group to find a partner to compare responses.

4. Ask the following questions of the entire group:

- Is violence always physical?
- Is violence ever justified within the family?
- Are there items on the worksheet that have absolutely no place within a family relationship?

5. Write the responses to the last question on a piece of newsprint. When the list is complete, ask participants if all agree with the items recorded.

6. Distribute copies of "Forms of Abuse" found on page 33. Take a moment to make any additions or deletions in light of the group's discussion on what domestic violence is or is not.

7. Before proceeding into further study on child abuse, acquaintance rape and date rape, spouse abuse, and/or elder abuse, ask the group to join in a moment of prayer for all those affected by overt and subtle forms of domestic violence.

Domestic Violence Worksheet

The following is a list of actions or experiences that occur in family settings. In the blank next to each word, rate how hurtful or abusive you think these actions are.

1 — Extremely abusive
2 — Abusive
3 — May or may not be abusive
4 — Usually is not abusive
5 — Not abusive at all

_____Yelling

_____Sarcasm

_____Spanking

_____Verbal Insults

_____Nagging

_____Hitting

_____Forced Sexual Relations

_____Insolence

_____Rudeness

_____Withholding of Privileges

_____Beating with a Stick or Belt

_____Belittling

_____Teasing

_____Harm or Harassing of Pets

_____Threatening to Harm Self or Another

Forms of Abuse

Abuse may be defined as any behavior, whether expressed physically, psychologically, sexually, or in the destruction of the victim's property, that threatens to do harm or actually does harm within the marital or partner relationship. Such abuse is usually not a one-time occurrence, is minimized by the abuser and the victim, is cyclic, and escalates in severity over time. In the absence of intervention (seeking shelter, contacting law enforcement, etc.), the violence will continue and often results in death.

Physical Violence

Aggressive behavior done to the victim's body by the perpetrator. This includes pushing, shoving, kicking, slapping, punching, choking, biting, pinching, hair-pulling, hitting, burning, clubbing, stabbing, shooting, and threatening with a knife or gun. Sometimes particular areas of the body are targeted.

Sexual Violence

Physical attacks or abuse of the genital areas or breast. This includes unwanted touching or pinching of breasts, rape with objects, forced sexual activity with a third person, forced sexual relations accompanied by either physical violence or the threat of physical violence. This also includes marital rape.

Emotional/Psychological Violence

Assaults against a person's well-being by systematically degrading the victim's self-worth through name-calling, derogatory or demeaning comments; forcing the victim to perform humiliating, degrading acts; threats to harm or kill the victim or victim's family; controlling access to money, sleep habits, eating habits, social relations; and actions to imply the victim is "crazy."

Destruction of Property or Pets

A form of violence done without touching the victim's body. The assaults are made viciously on the victim by destroying personal belongings, family heirlooms, or the family pet. The property or pets of the victim is destroyed in a deliberate, targeted manner, and the psychological impact may be as devastating as a physical attack.

Suggested Session Plan on

O LORD, you will hear the desire of the meek;
  you will strengthen their heart,
      you will incline your ear
to do justice for the orphan and the oppressed,
  so that those from earth may strike terror no more.
                                                    —*Psalm 10:17–18*

Session Plan

You are encouraged to read the articles by Bos, Rifner, and Fortune before you lead this process. These articles provide valuable information about and insight into the problem of abuse and mistreatment. Please study the Session Plan in advance and make photocopies of necessary materials as needed.

1. Begin by reading the following Scripture. Ask the participants for any reflections on what they think Jesus is saying about how we are to treat one another, especially children.

> An argument arose among them as to which one of them was the greatest. But Jesus, aware of their inner thoughts, took a little child and put it by his side, and said to them, "Whoever welcomes this child in my name welcomes me, and whoever welcomes me welcomes the one who sent me; for the least among all of you is the greatest."
>
> —*Luke 9:46–48*

2. Review (or read aloud) the section "We Won't Let It Happen Here: Keeping Children Safe from Sexual Abuse" found on pp. 8–10. Then on newsprint, write the following:

- We are too trusting.
- We want to think the best of people and to welcome people into our midst.
- We are too quick to forgive.

If there are more than five in the group, place the participants in small groups. Ask the group(s) to discuss whether or not they agree with these statements and why.

3. Distribute copies of "Myths and Realities about Child Abuse" (see pp. 41–42). Ask the participants to get into pairs and discuss any myth they once believed in as a fact and why.

Allow time for volunteers to share their discussion with the whole group.

4. Show the video *Hear Their Cries.* (See p. 119 in the Resources section for information on this video.) After viewing, discuss the video using the questions in the accompanying study guide.

5. Summarize in your own words information concerning who abuses a child, found on pp. 38–40. Ask if there are any comments or surprises.

6. Tell the participants that a necessary part of preventing child sexual abuse is to educate our children about it. Children must be taught the difference between "OK" and "not OK" touches. They must be taught the "Stop! Go! Tell!" response to uncomfortable advances from anyone, even members of their own church family and immediate family.

Distribute copies of "Six Things Children Need to Know about Preventing Sexual Abuse," found on p. 44. Ask the participants to get into small groups and discuss one or more of these and provide at least three concrete ways that their congregation can help to teach them to the children. Once each group has finished, list these concrete ways on newsprint. Ask if there are other things that children need to be taught. Consider using this list to develop a preventing sexual abuse class for children.

7. Distribute copies of "Behavioral Indicators of Child Sexual Abuse," found on p. 43.

8. Consider doing a volunteer/staff training with your congregation. Ask if there are volunteers who would like to serve on a group to plan a workshop to help educate those in your congregation, especially those who are involved with children and youth. See "A Model for Child Abuse Prevention Education," developed by Susan Keil Smith of the Presbyterian Child Advocacy Network in Appendix A, pp. 101–111.

9. Close by reading the following excerpt from *Surely Heed Their Cry*.

In 1 Cor. 12:26 we are reminded that we are all members of the body of Christ; if "one member suffers, all suffer together with it." As people of God, we are responsible to and for each other. . . .

As representatives of Christ to each other, we have a unique calling and opportunity: we must act to end suffering, to prevent further harm, and to be God's agents for healing the brokenness in our midst, as we minister with the victim and/or survivor of abuse, the abuser, and the others affected. Our task as communities of faith is to demonstrate that we can be trustworthy; we can be a place where children are not betrayed, where their suffering is not ignored, and where true redemption and reconciliation is continually offered. Through our actions, God can provide hope and redemption to those affected by the sin of child abuse.[1]

Who Abuses a Child?

No particular profile can be used to predict a parent or caregiver who will abuse a child.

Abuse occurs in all segments of society, regardless of economic status, race or ethnicity, or educational level. Many who physically abuse or neglect children in their care do love these children, but they feel overwhelmed by their circumstances and feel unable to cope with the stresses they are experiencing. Children are sometimes convenient targets for anger or neglect; they have little hope of defending themselves against the power of an adult.

However, some of the identified risk factors for abuse and neglect by parents or other main caregivers include the following:

- *Short- or long-term crises in the family.* Dealing with any kind of stress, whether financial, emotional, or physical, can place parents and caregivers at increased risk for lashing out at their children or neglecting them. Such crises can include job loss, divorce or marital discord, health problems, and any other crisis that threatens to overwhelm a family.

- *Problems with alcohol or other drug use.* Though alcohol and other drugs do not cause abusive behavior, such substances can lessen the ability of a parent or caregiver for self-control and appropriate management of anger. Also people with drug problems are less likely to give proper attention to a child's ongoing needs. Alcohol and other drugs are estimated to be factors in about half of all reported cases of child abuse and neglect.

- *The experience of abuse and neglect as children.* Most who are abused do not grow up to be abusive. However, many people who abuse children in their care were, themselves, abused as children. People with a history of abuse must seek out alternative methods of discipline and coping mechanisms to replace what they learned. If they do not learn other, healthier patterns, they are likely to be abusive to their own children or those in their care.

---

[1] *Surely Heed Their Cry,* pp. 11–12.

- *A real or perceived isolation from sources of support.* [People who abuse] may be alienated or separated from extended family and may not be part of other kinds of ongoing supportive interaction with other adults.

- *Low self-esteem.* [People who abuse] are likely to feel negatively about themselves and their ability to succeed in the world and in their relationships.

- *Perception of a child as "different."* As a result of an unplanned pregnancy, difficult birth, or an actual disability, parents and caregivers may feel an added burden in caring for the child. This feeling, regardless of its logic or fairness, places the child at increased risk for abuse by that caregiver. Children with disabilities are more vulnerable than other children; they are less likely to be able to defend themselves or tell someone else about their experience of abuse.

- *Inappropriate expectations for the child.* The parents or caregivers may not understand the limitations of children at various states of development or may have unfair or unspoken expectations that the child cannot fulfill.

- *Rigid or moralistic attitudes and behavior.* Caregivers or parents may have difficulty accepting the mistakes of children. Expectations may be such that a child could never begin to meet them.

- *Low impulse control.* People who abuse children have underdeveloped skills for appropriate direction of their anger and for understanding the consequences of their actions. This is not to say that they are not able to learn these skills. It is possible that they have not been made to face consequences of their actions in the past, or they may never have learned how to cope with feelings, such as anger, appropriately.

Who Sexually Abuses a Child?

The risk factors associated with child physical and emotional abuse may also indicate persons at risk for sexually abusing a child. Because sexual abuse of children has only recently become recognized as an area of concern desperately needing research and study, there is much debate among experts regarding whether an "offender profile" exists. Most experts agree, however, that certain characteristics tend to be present in those persons who sexually abuse children, whether they are parents, family members, friends, or others.

- *An ability to manipulate convincingly.* Because secrecy is essential to the offender's ability to continue abusing, this person is skilled at lying and covering up anything that might expose this behavior. Sexual abusers, in outward appearances, may be successful and popular; they may be the last people you would suspect of sexual abuse of children. These outward characteristics help them to continue their abuse in secret.

- *An inability to meet intimacy or sexual needs appropriately.* Though many sexual abusers are married and may appear outwardly well-adjusted, they do not know how to get their needs met appropriately in mutual relationships with other adults. They find it easier to get needs met by children, who do not have the power to reject them.

- *The possession of power greater than the victim.* Obviously, adult sex offenders hold considerable power over any child. Some children are abused, however, by other, older children or youth who have the ability to exercise power over them. Often, these children who abuse have been or are currently being abused themselves. Research indicates that about half of adult offenders began abusing in their teens.

- *Continued perpetration of abuse without intervention to stop it.* As the statistics indicate, it is rare that a sex offender offends once or even with a single victim. Typically, perpetrators continue to abuse until intervention takes place.

It is important to remember that both males and females can and do sexually abuse children, just as both males and females are the victims of child abuse. Most cases do involve male perpetrators, but current research indicates that the number of female perpetrators has been underestimated. It is also important to know that the sex of the victim of sexual abuse does not necessarily reflect the abuser's sexual preference; most boys (and girls) are abused by adult, heterosexual males.[2]

---

[2]Bonnie Glass MacDonald, *Surely Heed Their Cry: A Presbyterian Guide to Child Abuse Prevention, Intervention, and Healing.* Louisville: Presbyterian Church (U.S.A.), 1993, pp. 17–18, 20. Used by permission.

Myths and Realities about Child Abuse

Myth: Sexual abuse only happens to girls.

Reality: One out of every three or four girls is sexually assaulted before they turn eighteen. However, at least one out of every five boys will be abused during his youth.

Myth: Child molesters are "dirty old men."

Reality: Unfortunately, society still believes in the stereotype about the dirty old man, waiting to lure a child off so he could abuse him or her. While the majority of offenders are male, women also molest children. Often prevention efforts focus on "don't talk to strangers." However, the fact is that the most danger for children is in their own home. Sixty percent of child sexual assaults take place in the victim's or offender's home. Eighty to ninety percent of sex offenders are known to the child.

Myth: Most perpetrators are mentally ill.

Reality: Most perpetrators do not have prior criminal records and are often viewed as "good family men." Frequently, in incestuous situations, the family is active in religious organizations. Studies portray the average perpetrator as being average in intelligence and education.

Myth: Sex offenders are homosexuals.

Reality: Most sex offenders are heterosexual males. Reports show that male offenders attracted to young boys typically state that they are uninterested in or repulsed by adult homosexual relationships, but find young boy's feminine characteristics and absences of secondary sexual characteristics, such as body hair, appealing.

Myth: Victims of sexual abuse are most often adolescents.

Reality: In "Sexually Victimized Children," David Finkelhar states that preadolescents are the most likely victims of a perpetrator. The average age of a sexually abused child is eight years old, although it is not uncommon for abuse to begin at a much earlier age.

Myth: Incest offenders only molest children in their own family.

Reality: Research indicates that up to 50 percent of incest offenders also molest children outside their families. It is believed that there are between 10 million and 25 million adults now living in the United States who are survivors of childhood sexual abuse.

Myth: If we don't talk about it, the child will forget.

Reality: Children who are sexually victimized tend to suffer extreme levels of guilt and self-blame as they move into adulthood. Studies show that some children will reexperience the trauma with symptoms of anxiety, fear, phobias, depression, suicide, substance abuse, self-destructive behavior, nightmares, clinging behavior, and vulnerability to future victimization. It is important to find ways to talk about it.

Myth: Children make up stories.

Reality: Statistics indicate that only two out of two hundred children who claimed to be victims of incest were lying. Professionals who treat child victims have found that the trauma of disclosing the abuse is so devastating that lying is seldom a factor. Children typically do not have the experience or vocabulary to accurately describe adult sexual activity, nor do they lie to get themselves into trouble.

Myth: The lack of physical violence in child abuse means children are willing sexual participants.

Reality: The notion that a child is sexually provocative is a myth that puts the blame on the victim. A child's behavior is in no way an explanation for the abusive actions of an adult offender. Often verbal threats and coercion are used to force children to participate.

Myth: Victims of child abuse do not treat other children in the way they were treated.

Reality: The most common characteristic of child sexual abuse is that the child perpetrates abuse on other children. According to the National Institute of Mental Health, at least 300,000 young people who were abused, sexually abused other children.

Behavioral Indicators of Child Sexual Abuse

It is critical to remember that no symptoms may be present. While there may be no signs that clearly indicate abuse, it is just as likely that several of these signs could be exhibited in any other crisis, such as divorce or death.

General Indicators

- irritability, sleep difficulties, feeding disturbances
- bedwetting
- overly compliant behavior
- acting-out, aggressive behavior
- compulsive behavior
- learning difficulties
- pseudomature behavior
- hints about sexual activity
- persistent and inappropriate sexual play with peers or toys or with themselves, or sexually aggressive behavior with others
- detailed and age-inappropriate understanding of sexual behavior (especially by young children)
- arriving early at school and leaving late, with few, if any, absences
- poor peer relationships or inability to make friends
- lack of trust, particularly with significant others
- nonparticipation in school and social activities
- inability to concentrate in school
- sudden drop in school performance
- extraordinary fears of males (in cases of male perpetrator and female victim)
- seductive behavior with males (in cases of male perpetrator and female victim)
- running away from home
- sleep disturbances
- regressive behavior
- withdrawal
- alcohol and drug abuse, other self-destructive behavior (e.g., eating disorders)
- clinical depression
- suicidal feelings

Specific Indicators

- specifically sexual symptoms
- somatic symptoms with sexual content
- physical symptoms
- running away from home
- bizarre degree of jealousy and possessiveness on father's part
- verbal reports of sexual abuse
- children who sexually abuse other children

Six Things Children Need to Know about Preventing Sexual Abuse

1. Children must be taught about "OK" and "not OK" touches. They need to be encouraged to trust their own feelings about what touches feel uncomfortable.

2. Children need to understand what is meant by their "private parts," the areas of the body covered by their swimsuits.

3. Children need to be taught that their bodies are their own; they have the right to say no to people (adults or other children) who touch them for their own gratification and cause them to feel uncomfortable, even if that person is someone they are supposed to trust, such as a family member, a teacher, a minister, or a childcare provider.

4. Children can be helped to practice saying no and also to name some trusted adults that they could tell if someone's touching has made them uncomfortable. They must be encouraged to tell an adult if they are being abused or if they are uncomfortable with the way someone touches them. They should keep telling until someone believes them.

5. Children should be helped to understand the difference between secrets and surprises. If they are uncomfortable about keeping a secret, they should tell a trusted adult.

6. The shame and guilt for abuse belong to the abuser; children are never to blame. Children can be taught to be assertive and careful, but they cannot always prevent abuse, and they should never be made to feel that they caused the abuse. The best thing that children can do is tell someone.

Suggested Session Plan on

Acquaintance Rape and Date Rape

O LORD, you will hear the desire of the meek;
   you will strengthen their heart,
     you will incline your ear
to do justice for the orphan and the oppressed,
   so that those from earth may strike terror no more.
       —*Psalm 10:17–18*

Session Plan

You are encouraged to read the articles by Bos, Fortune, and Parrot before you lead this process. These articles provide valuable information about and insight into the problem of abuse and mistreatment. Please study the Session Plan in advance and make photocopies of necessary materials as noted.

1. Ask for a volunteer to read aloud the section "Socialization That Is Conducive to a Date Rape Occurrence" on p. 11. Then ask for general discussion about the reading, using the following questions:

- Are you in agreement with what was read? Why or why not?
- Are things changing in terms of how women and men are being socialized today? How?
- What role do you feel the church plays in women/men socialization?

2. Ask for a volunteer to read aloud the section "Blaming the Victim" on pp. 11–12. Then ask for general discussion about the reading using the following questions:

- Are you in agreement with what was read? Why or why not?
- In your community, do you feel there is a "Blame-the-Victim Syndrome"?
- If so, is there something that your congregation can do to change this situation?

3. Read aloud to the group "Some Facts You Should Know about Rape" on p. 49. After each one is read, ask for any comments or discussions about that particular statistic.

4. Discuss the following questions:

- Why is it important to look at the issue of sexual assault within a Christian context?
- How has the church perpetuated walls of silence around this issue?
- How can the socialization of men and women lead to sexual assault?
- How do you feel the church views sexuality? (male sexuality; female sexuality; sex within marriage; sex outside of marriage; homosexual couples; single couples)
- What is your experience of the church's view of sexual violence? the perpetrator of violence? the survivor of the violence?
- Where does the Bible tell of incidents of sexual violence? What is the attitude toward it? in the Old Testament? in the New Testament? (See the story of Hagar [Genesis 16, 21]; the story of Tamar [2 Samuel 13]; the story of the unnamed woman [Judges 19:1–30]; the story of Jepthath's daughter [Judges 11:29–40].)
- Discuss the emotional aftermath of assault: fear, denial, difficulty in trusting others, violations, anger, fear to be alone, fear to be with others, guilt, numbness, feeling dirty, grief.
- Now that trust is violated, can it be restored? How?
- How is God's grace experienced after sexual assault?
- Is it possible to forgive the perpetrator, God, oneself? If so, how?

5. Distribute copies of "How the Presbyterian Church (U.S.A.) Has Responded," found on p. 51. Ask the participants to comment on concrete, visible ways they see or know their denomination to be upholding these responses.

6. Distribute copies of "Suggestions for Action," found on p. 52. Consider what concrete actions groups and/or individuals can take to respond to this form of violence against women.

7. Close with prayer using one of the benedictions from the worship materials on pp. 88–98 of this resource.

Some Facts You Should Know about Rape

- One of every four female college students will be sexually attacked before graduating; one in seven will be raped.
- One rape is reported every three minutes in the United States.
- Only 10 to 25 percent of rapes are ever reported.
- Eighty-five percent of rapes occur between people who know each other (friend, neighbor, family member, and so on).
- Fifty percent of rapes occur in the victim's home.
- Approximately 28 percent of dating individuals will be involved in intimate violence at some point during their dating lives.
- Approximately 30 percent of all females under the age of twenty have experienced some kind of dating violence before they are adults.

Myths and Realities about Rape

There are many myths and beliefs in our society about rape. Unfortunately, these beliefs often permit rape or implicitly give the rapist permission for his actions. In order to prevent sexual assault, we need to understand what rape is and what it isn't.[1]

Myth: A woman who gets raped deserves it, especially if she agreed to go to the man's house or ride in his car.

Reality: No one, male or female, deserves to be raped. Being in a man's house or car does not mean a woman has agreed to have sex with him. Research has shown that the way a woman dresses or acts or behaves has very little to do with whether or not she is raped. Additionally, she does not "owe" the man sex, even if he has spent money on her.

Myth: If there's no gun or knife or if the woman doesn't fight back, it's not rape.

Reality: It's rape whether the rapist uses a weapon or his fists, verbal threats, drugs or alcohol, physical isolation, the victim's own diminished physical or mental state, or simply the weight of his body to overcome her. An individual is raped whenever forced to have sex against her will, whether she fought back or not. Not fighting back or screaming is more of an indication of fear than of "wanting it."

---

[1] This list is adapted from *Never Called It Rape* by Robin Warshaw as printed in *Lord, Hear Our Prayers: Domestic Violence Worship Resources* compiled by Kathy Shantz. Published by Mennonite Central Committee Canada, 1994, pp. 65–66. Used by permission.

Myth: It's not really rape if the victim isn't a virgin.

Reality: Rape is rape, even if the woman isn't a virgin and even if she willingly had sex with the man before.

Myth: Agreeing to kiss or neck or pet with a man means that a woman has agreed to have intercourse with him.

Reality: Everyone has the right to say "no" to sexual activity, regardless of what has preceded it, and to have that "no" respected.

Myth: When men are sexually aroused, they need to have sex and can't keep themselves from forcing sex on a woman.

Reality: Men don't physically need to have sex after becoming aroused any more than women do. Moreover, men are still able to control themselves even after becoming sexually excited.

Myth: Women lie about being raped, especially when they accuse the men they date or other acquaintances.

Reality: Rape really happens—to people you know, by people you know!

How the Presbyterian Church (U.S.A.) Has Responded

In 1979 the Council on Women and the Church (COWAC) submitted a report to the 191st General Assembly of the United Presbyterian Church of the United States of America. The report identified the rise of sexual and domestic violence in the U.S. and called on Christians to give compassionate and active responses to the needs of victims of rape. The report therefore urged the church to "strengthen its response to the issues of sexual and domestic violence" by

- Calling church members and judicatories to examine their attitudes toward the issue and its victims and removing all existing blocks to direct confrontation;
- Urging the presbyteries, seminaries, and training centers to provide educational opportunities to all those affected by rape;
- Instructing communication with all pastors and clerks to be aware of the need for competent counseling for both victims and assailants of sexual and domestic violence;
- Urging all presbyteries to "identify available community resources, applicable laws, and methods of intervention relating to crimes of sexual and domestic violence."

The 191st General Assembly adopted this document, calling sexual and domestic violence problems that affect all peoples, including Christians. It was determined that the church has a moral responsibility to the larger community "to be a witness against sexual and domestic violence." There are too many groups in society, the report adds, that are unwilling or unable to speak and act out a moral position. It is therefore up to the church to do its part in making clear that sexual and domestic violence are "profound" abuses that will not be accepted. The report concludes, "The goodness of God's creation is celebrated in healthy sexual sharing between mutually consenting equals in a context of respect, caring, and trust; it is denied when sexual activity takes place in a context of violence and exploitation."

Suggestions for Action

1. Become knowledgeable about your community.

- Is there a rape crisis center or hotline?
- Do the police deal with rape victims sensitively?
- Is there a safe shelter where both victims and children can be accommodated?
- Are clergypersons ready to help both victims and assailants?

2. If you are a college student, become knowledgeable and *active* on your campus.

- Are there support groups for women? If not, why not start one?
- Participate in "take back the night" vigils that show concern and solidarity with women who have been sexually attacked and/or raped.
- Are there escort services on campus? If not, urge your campus security to provide them.
- Post crisis numbers on school bulletin boards.

3. Volunteer to work at a local women's shelter or at a sexual assault or rape crisis center. They will provide the training needed to be helpful.

4. Vote and lobby. Be aware of which candidates support rape crisis centers and which take active roles in legislation that protects women's rights.

Write your representatives urging them to vote for legislation that will help address violence against women. Contact the Presbyterian Church (U.S.A.) Washington Office for more information about such legislation. Find out what your state legislature is doing to respond to violence against women.

5. Educate yourself and your community about violence against women. During National Domestic Violence Week or International Women's Day, bring in speakers, offer seminars, or stage a theatre production that dramatizes the issue of rape.

6. Organize a workshop on date rape using the information in this session.

7. Attend or sponsor a self-defense class for women.

Suggested Session Plan on

Spouse Abuse

O LORD, you will hear the desire of the meek;
   you will strengthen their heart,
      you will incline your ear
to do justice for the orphan and the oppressed,
   so that those from earth may strike terror no more.
            —*Psalm 10:17–18*

Session Plan

You are encouraged to read the articles by Bos, Fortune, and Rifner before you lead this process. These articles provide valuable information about and insight into the problem of abuse and mistreatment. Please study the Session Plan in advance and make photocopies of necessary materials as noted.

1. Open the study session by introducing yourself, and then ask participants to introduce themselves.

2. Ask participants to share something about themselves by describing a sacred or special place, a place where they encounter God's presence in their lives. Begin this process by describing a place that is special to you.

3. Read aloud or provide copies of the Scripture found on p. 63 to the participants to read silently.

4. Write on a chalkboard or newsprint, "What Is Spouse Abuse?" Ask participants to think of words or phrases that describe spouse abuse. Write their responses on the chalkboard or newsprint.

5. Divide the group into four small groups and distribute copies of "Forms of Abuse," p. 33, and "Myths and Realities about Spouse Abuse," pp. 59–60. Assign each small group one of the four types of spouse abuse listed on the first sheet. Ask each group to make a list of every violent act that would be connected to the type of abuse they have been assigned.

6. When they have completed their lists, ask each group to share with the larger group. Write the responses on the chalkboard or newsprint.

7. Ask someone to read the following list of abusive acts. Put a check by those already named on the newsprint. Add to the list any acts not already included.

- Grabbing or holding a person to keep him or her from leaving.
- Embarrassing a person in public or private.
- Subjecting a person to reckless driving.
- Hurting a person in a joking way—twisting arms, tickling, pulling, or pushing.
- Throwing objects at a person.
- Insisting on unwanted or uncomfortable touching.
- Hitting objects like a wall or a door.
- Constantly criticizing a person, name calling, or shouting.
- Withholding approval, appreciation, or affection to punish a person.
- Acting jealous about time spent with other people.
- Calling a person sexual names.
- Throwing or damaging a person's possessions.
- Kidnapping or injuring a person's pets.
- Pushing, shoving, slapping, hitting, kicking, or biting a person.
- Using weapons against a person.
- Forcing or coercing a person to have sex.
- Isolating a person from family, friends, or other contacts.
- Monitoring a person's telephone calls.
- Withholding money or monitoring expenditures.

Have the group discuss the following questions:

• Are there any items on the list that surprise you as being labeled abusive?
Why or why not?

• In your own life and the lives of people you know, how many of these acts
have you heard about or experienced?[1]

8. Ask three volunteers to read the dialogue "The Downward Spiral of Violence in the
Home," on pp. 64–66.

9. If the group is larger than five, divide participants into smaller groups. Ask each
group to appoint a recorder to write down the responses. Ask participants to discuss the
following questions:

• What forms of abuse have occurred in Grace and Stephen's story?
(Participants might want to check the list on the chalkboard or newsprint
to identify types of abuse.)

• What do you think is the cause of the violence?

• What steps could be taken to stop the escalation of violence?

10. Divide the group into two small groups. Distribute copies of "Profile of an Abuser"
on p. 62 to one group. Ask participants to think of Stephen in the dialogue that was just read
and answer the questions for discussion on the handout.

Distribute copies of "Characteristics and Behavior of Victims of Abuse" on p. 61 to the
second group. Ask participants to think of Grace in the dialogue that was just read and answer
the questions for discussion on the handout.

Gather the group back together and ask: Thinking about both the abusers and the
victims of abuse, in what ways does the church and society in general ignore or perhaps
perpetuate the cycle of abuse?

11. Tell participants that the church can play an important role in stopping the cycle of
violence and abuse in homes. Ask a participant to read aloud the following excerpt from
"Picking Up the Broken Pieces: Responding to Domestic Violence" by Marie Fortune. (The full
text is on pp. 13–19 of this resource.)

> The first [role] is pastoral. Our people are hurting. Families and individuals are being
> destroyed by violence. Children are growing up believing that daddy hitting mommy is
> just the way things are. Many women live with the fact that their home is the most
> dangerous place for them to be. People need to know that they can come to their church
> for support and information, and, when they come, they need to find church leaders
> prepared to assist them.
>
> The second is pragmatic: the issue of violence against women needs to be one of the
> priorities of a peacemaking agenda because it is a social issue that is personal and
> immediate in our lives right here. The fact that women and girls in our culture learn
> early that we have no right to bodily integrity, that we have no right to be free from
> bodily harm is a fact that has long been accepted as normal.

---

[1] Adapted from Sharon K. Youngs, *Confronting Domestic Violence: Not Just for Adults*. Louisville: Curriculum Publishing, Presbyterian
Church (U.S.A.), 1996.

When this piece has been read, distribute copies of "What Can the Church Do?" on p. 67. Then ask participants to brainstorm possible ways the congregation might respond pastorally or pragmatically. List these on newsprint marked "Pastoral" and "Pragmatic." Ask if there is a group of people who would like to work on further study and possible recommendations to session.

12. Close with the following prayer or choose one of the benedictions from the worship materials on p. 94 of this resource.

Compassionate and loving God, lend your ear to all who cry out to you in pain and affliction. Comfort and assure especially those who are victims of violence in their own homes. Give them strength to take flight like the dove, seeking shelter from the tempest. May your spirit of mercy and healing surround them, giving the promise of wholeness and renewal in your loving care.

God of love and justice, help us to hear the stories of lives broken by violence; give us courage to share our own. Nurture us and sustain us that some day all homes will be dwelling places for your love. In the name of our Savior, Jesus Christ. Amen.

Some Facts You Should Know about Spouse Abuse

- One incident of "wife beating" is reported every minute in the United States (three times higher than rape). This report represents less than 10 percent of all actual incidents.

- One out of every two women will experience some form of violence in relationships with other adults (spouse, lover) at some point in her life. (Dr. Lenore Walker)

- Sixty percent of couples will experience some degree of physical violence at some point in their relationship. (Murray Strauss, "Normative and Behavioral Aspects of Violence Between Spouses," unpublished, University of New Hampshire.)

- Domestic violence is the single major cause of injury to American women, exceeding rapes, mugging, and even auto accidents.

- Ninety-five percent of the victims of spouse abuse are women.

- Every fifteen seconds a woman is beaten.

- There are over four million reported cases of battered women each year.

- Fifty to eighty percent of women on welfare have been battered or are currently victims of abuse.

- A female victim is assaulted on the average of seven to ten times before she seeks assistance.

- More than 50 percent of homeless women left their homes to escape a battering situation.

- Sixty percent or more of Aid for Dependant Children recipients are current or past victims of domestic violence.

- Domestic violence is the most under reported crime in the United States.

- In a recent survey, over 50 percent of abused women lost at least three days of work a month due to abuse.

- Domestic violence costs American companies $3–5 billion, resulting from lost work time, including health care costs, high turnover, and low productivity.[2]

---

[2]Sources for facts: *Women and Violence: A Faith Perspective*, Justice for Women Working Group, 1994; *The "Safety Net" Saves Lives: Supporting Women and Families in the Face of Violence*, NOW Legal Defense Fund, 1996; and Jody Raphael, *Prisoners of Abuse: Domestic Violence and Welfare Receipt*, Taylor Institute, 1996.

Myths and Realities about Spouse Abuse

Myth: Stresses, such as money, a move, having a baby, or job problems are what cause a person to abuse his partner.

Reality: Everyone faces stress, but not everyone who is stressed resorts to abuse. Stress is not an excuse for abuse.

Myth: Abused women are basically masochistic and enjoy being abused; that's why they stay in abusive situations.

Reality: Victims stay in abusive situations because they feel trapped, not because they gain pleasure from abuse. The reasons most women stay in abusive relationships is because they are economically and/or emotionally dependent on the abuser. Many people will do almost anything to keep a marriage and family together. The community, family members, and even the church will sometimes encourage a person to stay.

Myth: Spouse abuse is a problem more commonly found in lower-class families.

Reality: Spouse abuse is a societal problem. It occurs within all classes, races, professions, and religious groups.

Myth: A woman provokes abuse by irritating or annoying her partner.

Reality: Some batterers report that provocative or irritating behavior caused them to abuse, but others report that nothing was done to provoke them. There is never a justifiable excuse to abuse.

Myth: Spouse abuse can be directly tied to alcoholism; only drunk men batter.

Reality: One-third of the perpetrators do not drink at all. One-third do have a drinking problem, but abuse whether drunk or sober. One-third abuse only when drunk. Alcohol and drug abuse can make domestic violence worse, but it doesn't cause it to happen.

Myth: "Uppity," assertive women are beaten more often than submissive women.

Reality: Some men report beating their partners because they were too assertive; other men report beating because their partners were too passive and agreeable. There seems to be a high incidence of battering in relationships where gender roles are narrowly defined and the man is completely in charge of the household.

Myth: Spouse abuse is a private family matter so outsiders should mind their own business.

Reality: Spouse abuse is a societal concern, with implications extending beyond the immediate family. There is ample evidence to suggest that patterns of violent behavior within the family are cyclic and will continue in succeeding generations of the family unless the cycle of violence is broken.

Myth: Men are abused by their partners as much as women.

Reality: Both men and women are abused by spouses, but there is not as much conclusive data on abuse of men because they tend not to report it. However, physical injury is more likely to occur in violence directed against women. Women generally have fewer options to leave an abusive relationship.

Characteristics and Behaviors of Victims of Abuse

What kind of person is abused? Contrary to what some would like to believe, there is not a "typical" profile of a victim of abuse. However, over 95 percent of victims of spouse abuse are women. They come from all cultural, racial, economic, and religious backgrounds. There are some typical behaviors and characteristics of victims of spouse abuse. These include the following:

- A lack of awareness of or dismissing the abuse.
- Economic dependence on the abuser.
- Fear of losing children if she leaves.
- Insecurity about being alone.
- Fear that she will be judged harshly by her faith community or family if she leaves.
- No other housing options.
- Inadequate job skills or training required to be financially independent.
- Hope that the abuser will change.
- Fear of retaliation.
- Feeling that the violence is at least partially her fault.

Often victims of abuse try very hard to hide the violence they are experiencing. There are some signs that might indicate the possibility of abuse. These include the following:

- Bruises or injuries for which the victim has vague explanations.
- Few or no friends.
- Abruptly ending phone calls.
- Asking permission or checking with partner prior to going shopping or out with friends.
- Gets frequent phone calls from partner while at work.
- Unexplained sadness for a time, followed by contentment, even happiness. Eventually the sadness returns.
- Dressing in long pants or long-sleeved clothing even when it is warm outside.
- Reluctance to join in extra activities, rarely staying after church or work.
- Edginess or unexplained nervousness.[3]

Discussion Questions

- Does Grace fit any of the characteristics or exhibit any of the behaviors listed?
- Why do you think it was so difficult for Grace to leave?

---

[3]Adapted from Patricia Riddle Gaddis, *Battered but Not Broken: Help for Abused Wives and Their Church Families*. Valley Forge: Judson Press, 1996.

Profile of an Abuser

Below is a list of characteristics of individuals who commit acts of domestic violence. While there is no "typical abuser," some or all of these characteristics may be visible.

- Ninety-five to ninety-seven percent are male.
- Is found in all socioeconomic and educational levels.
- Is found in all races and religions.
- Is young, middle-aged, or old.
- Exhibits signs of extreme jealousy and possessiveness of partner or date.
- Is emotionally dependent on partner or date (demands lots of "strokes").
- Has low self-esteem.
- Exhibits a pattern of blaming others, especially partner or date, for own problems.
- Has rigid role expectations of what women and men should be and do.
- Has derogatory or negative attitude toward women in general.
- Has poor self-image about being male.
- Has difficulty in being close to others.
- Has violent and/or explosive temper, especially about little things.
- Is more likely than not to have a history of abuse as a child or witnessed abuse of mother by father.
- Minimizes or denies abusive actions.
- Has difficulty in differentiating feelings; emotions, especially unpleasant ones such as fear and loneliness, are expressed as anger.
- Is slow to recognize own stress or frustration; lets it build up until it reaches explosion level.
- Feels entitled to have own way at the expense of others.[4]

Discussion Questions

- In what ways does Stephen fit the profile of an abuser?
- Do you know anyone, or have you ever experienced, these characteristics in yourself or another person?

---

[4]Adapted from Sharon K. Youngs, *Confronting Domestic Violence: Not Just for Adults.* Louisville: Curriculum Publishing, Presbyterian Church (U.S.A.), 1996.

Passages from Psalm 55

Give ear to my prayer, O God;
    do not hide yourself from my supplication.
My heart is in anguish within me,
    the terrors of death have fallen upon me.
Fear and trembling come upon me,
    and horror overwhelms me.
And I say, "O that I had wings like a dove!
    I would fly away and be at rest;
truly, I would flee far away;
    I would lodge in the wilderness;
I would hurry to find a shelter for myself
    from the raging wind and tempest."
It is not enemies who taunt me—
    I could bear that;
it is not adversaries who deal insolently with me—
    I could hide from them.
But it is you, my equal,
    my companion, my familiar friend,
with whom I kept pleasant company;
    we walked in the house of God with the throng.
My companion laid hands on a friend
    and violated a covenant with me
with speech smoother than butter,
    but with a heart set on war;
with words that were softer than oil,
    but in fact were drawn swords.
                    —Psalm 55:1, 4–8, 12–14, 20–21

The Downward Spiral of Violence in the Home—A Dialogue

Narrator: The story of Grace and Stephen is not a particularly unusual one. Grace grew up in a Christian family where Dad was the head of the household and Mom was a homemaker and very happy in that role.

Stephen's father was killed when he was very young. His mother had to work two jobs just to make ends meet. Since money was tight, his aunt watched him during the day. His aunt had a very short temper and spanked him frequently, especially if he upset his cousin. When his mom found out about the spankings, she felt bad but said there wasn't anything she could do. She told Stephen to be a little nicer and not upset his aunt or cousin.

Stephen's Mom did her best to provide for her son and never accepted a handout. They attended church every Sunday, and she made sure Stephen had opportunities to excel.

Reader 1: Hi. I'm Grace. I am twenty years old, married, and trying to figure out where my life went so wrong. I guess it started when I was sixteen. That was when I met Stephen in the youth group at church. He was older and absolutely wonderful. He was an excellent student and athlete, tall, and handsome. I couldn't believe it when he asked me out. We were the perfect couple. He was so kind to me and polite to my family. He played basketball with my brother, and my parents adored him. He was really active in youth group, leading Bible studies and working with younger youth. But best of all, he treated me like a princess! I had never had someone pay so much attention to me before. He wanted me to spend every free moment with him, and it was wonderful. Sometimes I missed friends of my own age, but they seemed to understand. He was just so cool. He had a full scholarship to the local university. Everyone was delighted when we announced our engagement. I couldn't wait to be Stephen's wife.

Reader 2: I am Stephen. I am a 26-year-old medical student, trying to figure out school and my life. It just doesn't seem to be going the way I planned. I guess it started when I met Grace. Her parents were well respected members of the church. I worked with her dad on a committee. She was younger than I, quiet and reserved, but absolutely beautiful. I guess it was love at first sight. I loved everything about her, her quiet nature, her looks, but I mostly loved the way she included me as a part of her family. I hated being away from her for even a moment.

Reader 1: Stephen and I married the summer after I graduated from high school. I began a job at a local bank to help with Stephen's college expenses. He was a pre-med student and showed great promise, but school was very expensive. Our first months of marriage were idyllic. I loved decorating our little apartment and making a home for Stephen. We spent all of our free time together. I guess it started going downhill in the fall when classes began again. Stephen's classes were really tough, and he spent all his spare time studying. I missed being with him, but I didn't say anything because he was under so much pressure. I spent more time with my family and friends from work. One night I came home after work to find Stephen destroying the apartment. He was crazy, ripping down the curtains I made, breaking dishes. I was scared to death, but I asked him what he was upset about. He grabbed me hard, put his face really close to mine, and said, "I refuse to live like a pig!" and stormed out of the apartment.

Reader 2: When Grace and I were married, it all seemed too good to be true. She worked full time at a bank while I took classes at the university and worked in the lab. Since I had more free time, I kept our apartment neat. I can't stand clutter. We spent every spare moment together because we knew things would get much busier in the fall when I was in school full time. I don't know what happened, but once school started Grace was never around anymore. I would come home and have no idea where she was. She was also really sloppy. I left for school before her and would come home to find her breakfast dishes in the sink and the bed unmade. One night, after a tough exam, I walked in the door and found the cereal bowl Grace had used on the counter. I just couldn't take all the clutter and lost my temper.

Reader 1: Stephen's behavior really scared me. I tried talking to my mother, but she pointed out that he wouldn't have been so angry if I were neater. I tried harder to keep everything neat and tidy, but it was as if Stephen was trying to find fault with everything I did. He would get infuriated when I did anything with my friends. He wanted me to be home whenever he was home. I kept thinking if I tried harder, things would get better. One night he came home late. I had kept dinner warm in the oven. He seemed really quiet. I served him his plate. He took one bite, picked up the plate, and hurled it at me, yelling, "I refuse to eat this overcooked garbage!" He went into the bedroom, slammed the door, and stayed there the rest of the night. The corner of the plate hit my cheek and left a terrible bruise.

Reader 2: It seemed like Grace would just get on my nerves sometimes after we were married. One night I stopped by a buddy's place and had a couple of beers before heading home. When I came in, I could tell that Grace had been crying, but she didn't complain. She just put dinner on the table and asked me what I wanted to drink. As I sat, I realized she had gone to great trouble and expense to prepare a pleasant dinner, but it was all dried out. It was almost as if she was being nice to annoy me. Something in me just snapped, and I threw the plate at her. That Sunday she said she wasn't feeling well and told me to go to church without her. I wonder if she was afraid someone would ask her about the bruise on her face. I realized then that maybe I need to watch my behavior when I have a few drinks.

Reader 1: After the incident with the plate, Stephen was wonderful. He brought flowers home after church and offered to fix dinner that night. It was like it used to be for several weeks. He treated me so gently. I thought everything would get back to the way it had been before his outbursts began. However, it didn't. Stephen was very concerned about our financial status and kept control of our income. He received a small salary from his part-time job in the lab, and my job at the bank paid most of our bills. He gave me a weekly allowance for personal expenses. It wasn't much, but if I skipped lunch, I had a little left over. I was shopping with my mother one day and saw a beautiful dress on sale. I had almost enough to pay for it, and I needed a new dress for work and church. My mother gave me the ten extra dollars needed to pay for it. When I brought it home, Stephen was studying. I tried the dress on and showed him, thinking he would be proud of my thrift. Instead, he blew up again. He told me I looked like a cheap little "whore" and I had no business spending money on clothes like that. I tried explaining to him that I had saved money from my allowance and my mom had helped, but that just incited him more. He got up, came over, and tried ripping the dress off me. Then he slapped me, threw me on the couch, and tried to make love to me. I was crying so hard that he just slapped me again and left.

Reader 2: Once Grace really got under my skin. I was studying one day while she was out shopping with her Mom. She came home with a new dress. We were not in a position to buy clothes, and I was infuriated that she would buy something without consulting me. Then she told me her mom had helped pay for it and I lost it. I told her that I refused to take handouts from anybody. Couldn't she see how she hurt my pride? I let her know who's boss, and she just started crying so I left.

Narrator: The cycle of violence continued to escalate between Grace and Stephen. To the outside world, the couple were a happily married young couple with a great future. There were long periods of calm when Stephen was very tender and caring for Grace, but eventually the violence would erupt again, more brutal than the last episode. Grace retreated from her family and friends. Seeing them seemed to trigger an outburst, and it was difficult to explain away the black eyes, cuts, and bruises. Stephen thought that things would get better if they had a baby. Grace knew she wasn't ready to bring a child into her violent world so she secretly continued taking birth control pills. When Stephen discovered the pills, he beat Grace so badly she was hospitalized. The loving and devoted Stephen, now a respected intern at the hospital, refused to leave his injured wife's bedside. No one questioned where her wounds had come from, but marveled at Stephen's compassion and faithfulness.

What Can the Church Do?

The following are suggested responses to family violence:

1. Invite family violence prevention advocates to teach how to detect cases of abuse. When you know or suspect abuse or neglect, report it to the proper authorities.

2. Provide counsel and support to the abused. It is important that clergy, who may not have experience with abuse cases, know community services to which victims may be referred for help.

3. Provide pastoral concern for the abuser and encourage the perpetrator of the violence to seek skilled professional help.

4. Do not attempt to counsel a couple together when there is violence in the relationship.

5. In wife-battering cases, which are usually repetitive and go on for years, continue to be caring, supportive, and pastoral, even if the wife is unable to leave. This may mean providing financial assistance to a battered woman and her children.

6. Establish or sponsor a self-help group for families involved in child abuse.

7. Establish or sponsor a self-help group for adults who were sexually abused as children.

8. Establish or expand the church's family ministries program to include parenting classes, a family support network, and other services as needed and as feasible. It may also be helpful if the church affirms a broader concept of family than that of the traditional nuclear family. If factors prohibit the church from establishing some needed service, join with other churches in offering the service.

9. Have an adult study group plan a four-to-six-week study of violence and prevention of violence in the family, using this resource guide.

10. Volunteer to work at a local women's shelter or at a sexual assault or rape crisis center. They will provide the training needed to be helpful.

11. Open your home as a safe house where women and children can seek refuge in time of crisis. Various community groups coordinate safehouse programs and will train and prepare you to provide this service.

12. Encourage clergy and laypeople to secure more indepth training to be able to minister to abused people, many of whom have theological questions and doubts about their faith.

13. Have available at the church public service pamphlets and brochures about the various types of family violence and services to those involved in the violence. Post crisis numbers on the church bulletin board.

14. During National Domestic Violence Week in October, select family violence prevention as a sermon topic.

15. Stage a theater production that dramatizes the issues involved in family violence. Follow the presentation with an audience discussion.

16. Find out what your state is doing to respond to family violence. Determine where gaps exist in preventive services and support legislation that provides needed services.

17. Contribute financial support and services to families in crisis and to community agencies that respond to family violence.

18. Promote passage of legislation that seeks to improve the economic status of women (e.g., pay equity).

19. Offer seminars on the legal alternatives for abused spouses and family members and for elderly abused people.

20. Establish a voluntary assistance program or volunteer with a community program to provide services for the elderly and relief for people who care for the elderly.

Suggested Session Plan on

O Lord, you will hear the desire of the meek;
   you will strengthen their heart,
      you will incline your ear
to do justice for the orphan and the oppressed,
   so that those from earth may strike terror no more.
                              —*Psalm 10:17–18*

Study Process

You are encouraged to read the three articles by Bos, Fortune, and Robb before you lead this process. These articles provide valuable information about and insight into the problem of abuse and mistreatment. Please study the Session Plan in advance and make photocopies of necessary materials as noted.

1. Read aloud the following statement to the group:

"For most older adults, life is immeasurably enhanced by their relationship with family members. At no other time of life, save perhaps for childhood, does the family play such a pivotal role."[1]

Then ask the following:

- Do you agree or disagree with this statement? Why?
- If you agree, why do you think the family plays such a pivotal role?

List the answers to the last question on newsprint or chalkboard.

2. Read aloud to the group "Some Facts You Should Know about Elder Abuse" on p. 74 or consider writing them out in advance on chalkboard or newsprint and posting them on the wall.

Ask the group if there were any facts that surprised them or if there are any general comments they would like to make.

3. Read the following statements aloud. Have the group discuss whether the statement is true or false. Then read the comment following the statement to clarify the answer.

- The most common form of psychological abuse is rejection or simply ignoring elderly people.

   True. This kind of treatment conveys that elderly persons are worthless and useless to others. Elderly persons may subsequently regress and become increasingly dependent on others, who tend to resent the imposition and demands on their time and lifestyles. The pattern becomes cyclical: the more regressed the person becomes, the greater the dependence.[2]

- Individuals with Alzheimer's disease and other forms of dementia have a greater risk for physical abuse than elderly persons with other illnesses.

   True. Because these illnesses result in a high burden on the caregiver and subsequent depression of the caregiver, individuals with Alzheimer's disease and other forms of dementia have a greater risk for physical abuse. Living with and providing care to a confused elderly person are difficult, round-the-clock tasks that often exhaust family members. Family stress increases as members must work harder to fulfill their other responsibilities in addition to the needs of the elderly person.[3]

- Statistics show that 4 percent of senior citizens suffer from some form of abuse, neglect, or exploitation.

---

[1] Joseph J. Gallo, William Reichel, and Lillian M. Anderson, *Handbook of Geriatric Assessment*, second edition. Gaithersburg, MD: Aspen Publishers, Inc., 1995.

[2] Jacquelyn Campbell and Kären Landenburger, "Violence and Human Abuse," in *Community Health Nursing: Promoting Health of Aggregates, Families, and Individuals*, eds. M. K. Stenhope and J. Lancaster. St. Louis: Mosby Year Books, 1996, p. 743.

[3] "Violence in Human Abuse," p. 744.

True. Studies as recent as 1994 report that 4 percent of elderly people suffer from some sort of abuse. However, it is believed that similar to spouse abuse and child abuse, most cases of elder abuse go unreported.

- Five percent of elders are institutionalized; the rest either live alone or with family members.

True. Women, wives, daughters, daughters-in-law, sisters, or other female relatives represent more than 70 percent of all caregivers. Elderly men are generally cared for by their wives, whereas elderly women rely on their adult children. Family members in general prefer to provide care rather than to institutionalize their relatives.[4]

- Abuse of older adults by a family member is a recent phenomenon.

False. There is evidence from antiquity that abuse occurred throughout the ages, including idealized family times in the nineteenth century when, in an agricultural society, three-generation families commonly lived together. Evidence from sermons and court documents supports that often older adults were victimized, usually by family members, and that often the incentive for keeping grandparents in the home was to assure the transfer of property.[5]

- Negative behavior patterns observed in some older adults can be attributed to "bereavement overload" that is due to the various losses in their lives.

True. The aging process is characterized by various losses: loss of job, income, friends or family through death or moving; declining health; death or disability of their spouse; and losses of roles that accompany other losses. A tie with another person can make the critical difference between satisfaction and unhappiness.[6]

- For those persons who still live independently, the average family provides about twenty-five hours a week of special attention.

True. The average family spends about twenty-five hours per week providing special attention—shopping, laundry or dry cleaning, housecleaning, socializing, and so on.[7]

- Parent-caring is becoming a major source of stress in family life.

True. Bernice Neugarten stated in 1980, "Large numbers of families . . . are going too far in caring for older people, stripping themselves of economic, social, and emotional resources to do so. In fact, one recent study showed that parent-caring is becoming a major source of stress in family life. The institutionalization of a family member usually comes only after the family has already done everything possible for them to do."[8]

---

[4]Patricia C. Birchfield, "Elder Health," in *Community Health Nursing: Promoting Health of Aggregates, Families, and Individuals.* Eds. M. K. Stenhope and J. Lancaster. St. Louis: Mosby Year Books, 1996, pp. 591–92.

[5]Richard J. Ham and Philip D. Sloan, *Primary Care Geriatrics: A Case-Based Approach.* 2nd edition. St. Louis: Mosby Year Book, 1992, p. 467.

[6]"Elder Health," p. 592.

[7]*Domestic Mistreatment,* p. 1.

[8]*Domestic Mistreatment,* p. 1.

- Many families tend toward the belief that home care is the "best" alternative, and they may offer it in response to a sense of duty or guilt, rather than as a logical choice among potential options.

True. "Family members too frequently fail to understand or investigate [all] the options before they are confronted with a personal crisis and initiate a long period of home care. It is not unusual for adult sons or daughters, age 50 to 70, to accept in-home responsibility for 85- to 90-year-old parents, uncles, aunts, or siblings. In many cases the caregivers are only slightly more able than the dependents."[9]

4. Ask the group members to get into small groups. Provide for each group a copy of "Categories of Mistreatment," p. 75, and a case study (case studies are located on pp. 76–78). After each group has had time to discuss its case study, gather the groups together, and have a person from each group summarize the case study and their discussion.

5. Tell the group that the key to help eliminate the problem of violence and mistreatment of elder persons is prevention. Distribute copies of "Towards Prevention," pp. 79–81, to each person. Spend a few moments allowing the group to read through it.

Then ask the participants to get into three groups, each taking one of the three categories: individuals, families, communities. Ask each group to carefully look at the Dos and Don'ts in their assigned category and, based on what is listed there, choose three or four points of ways the church could be supportive by helping to make the "Do" or the "Don't" a reality.

Have the groups share with the total group their suggestions. List these on newsprint or chalkboard.

6. Have the group choose two or three items from the list and brainstorm to come up with a concrete plan for taking action to educate and help eliminate the mistreatment and abuse of elder persons. Consider sharing these with the church's session for endorsement and implementation.

---

[9]*Domestic Mistreatment*, p. 2.

Some Facts You Should Know about Elder Abuse

- Persons over eighty-five make up the fastest growing segment of the population of the United States.
- Children who find themselves caring for elderly parents may themselves be elderly.
- One in ten persons over sixty-five has a child who is at least sixty-five.
- Most often, the caregiver is a woman in her sixties caring for her mother.
- Because more persons are living to advanced age, the average woman can expect to spend more years caring for an elderly parent than her counterpart in 1990.
- The trend toward smaller families (meaning there are fewer adult children to serve as caregivers) further strains the support system of the older person.
- Seventy-two percent of primary caregivers are women. Of these female caregivers, 29 percent are daughters of the older person and 23 percent are wives of the older person.
- All fifty states, the District of Columbia, Guam, and the Virgin Islands have legislature protecting elderly persons.

Some Signs and Symptoms of Mistreatment or Abuse

In Caregivers

New self-neglect
Conflicting stories
Mounting resentment
Excusing failure
Shifting blame
Aggressive/defensive behavior
Substance abuse
Unusual fatigue
New affluence
New health problems
Preoccupation/depression
Withholding food/medication

In Older Persons

Increasing depression
Anxiety
Withdrawn/timid
Hostile
Unresponsive
Confused
Physically injured
New poverty
Longing for death
Vague health complaints
Anxious to please
Shopping for physicians

There are other signs and symptoms, and not all of those listed by themselves indicate mistreatment, neglect, or abuse. But if any seem to increase in number or severity in a domestic setting, it may indicate trouble. By watching for some of these signs and symptoms of stress or mistreatment, you may be able to initiate actions to reduce or prevent the situation from deteriorating.[10]

---

[10]Richard L. Douglass, *Domestic Mistreatment of the Elderly: Towards Prevention.* Criminal Justice Services of America Association of Retired Persons, 601 East Street, NW, Washington, DC 20049, 1992, p. 1. Used by permission.

Categories of Mistreatment

Passive Neglect

The unintentional failure to fulfill a caretaking obligation; there is no conscious or willful attempt to inflict physical or emotional distress on the older person. Examples: non-provision of food or health-related services because of the caregiver's infirmity, laziness, or inadequate skills, knowledge, or understanding of the necessity of prescribed or other essential services.

Psychological Abuse

The infliction of mental anguish. Examples: demeaning, name calling, treating as a child, insulting, ignoring, frightening, humiliating, intimidating, threatening, isolating.

Material (Financial) Abuse

The illegal or unethical exploitation and/or use of funds, property, or other assets belonging to the older person.

Active Neglect

The intentional failure to fulfill a caretaking obligation, including a conscious and willful attempt to inflict physical or emotional stress or injury on the older person. Examples: deliberate abandonment, deliberate denial of food or health-related services, depriving of dentures or eyeglasses.

Physical Abuse

The infliction of physical pain or injury or physical coercion (confinement against one's will). Examples: slapping, bruising, sexually molesting, cutting, lacerating, burning, physically restraining, pushing, shoving.[11]

---

[11]*Domestic Mistreatment*, pp. 3–4.

Case Studies

Martin's Story

When Martin was diagnosed with Alzheimer's disease at the age of 81, he moved into the home of his great-nephew, Frank, who was the only relative living nearby. Martin's children all lived in other states and visited only occasionally.

Uncle Martin and Frank had always been close, but Frank's wife and three teenaged children had never really developed a relationship with Martin. Although it was Frank who had invited Martin to live with them, the rest of the family took on the brunt of the responsibility since Frank worked long hours and frequently traveled with his job. One of the daughters had to give up her bedroom for Uncle Martin and move in with her sister.

Frank's wife, Mary, found it very difficult to get out of the house at all during the day because Martin could not be left unsupervised without causing problems around the house. Mary began to resent the restrictions on her time. When she did go out, she left Martin locked in his bedroom from which she removed most of his belongings.

The family developed tremendous resentment toward Uncle Martin and began to express it in name-calling, threats, and accusations, especially when Frank was away from home. A neighbor heard several episodes of shouting but did not intervene. Martin's doctor noticed that Martin was becoming increasingly confused and that he suffered many bruises, but he attributed those things to Martin's age and illness.

Finally, during one particularly violent shouting match, Martin became so frightened that he ran out of the house, became disoriented, and wandered around the streets all night before being found by the police.[12]

Discuss the following questions:

1. What types of violence or mistreatment are evident in this story?

2. What measures could have been taken to prevent the violence or mistreatment?

Betty's Story

Betty, a 78-year-old widow, lost her husband four years ago. She did the best she could to take care of herself and her needs, but she did get lonely. Many days would pass between the times she would see her daughter's family who lived about an hour away. When Tom, her son-in-law, came and asked her to move in with them, she was very excited. She thought how nice and comforting it would be to live with family once again.

After the first couple of months, her daughter, Anne, had a discussion with Betty, saying that she and Tom felt it would be best if they "helped" her by cashing, depositing, and managing all of her income. Betty knew of no reason to disagree. After all, they were providing a place for her to live with them.

Anne and Tom would cash her checks and take out a portion to cover Betty's groceries, utility usage, and the like, and deposit the rest. Betty began to notice from her checkbook that the deposits were getting to be less and less. Unbeknownst to Betty, Tom and Anne were in substantial debt and finding it hard to meet their monthly payments. When Betty confronted Tom asking for an explanation as to why her deposits were getting less and less, he told her to shut up and be grateful that they provided a roof over her head.

Discuss the following questions:

1. What types of violence or mistreatment are evident in this story?

2. What measures could have been taken to prevent the violence or mistreatment?

[12]Vera K. White, *Peacemaking in a Violent World*. Louisville: The Presbyterian Peacemaking Program, 1995, p. 8. To order call 800/524–2612 and request #70–350–95–289. Cost: $.75.

Jake's Story

Jake is an 80-year-old man, widowed for six years. He admitted it was getting harder and harder for him to get around. His eyesight was getting bad enough that he thought he'd best not drive anymore.

Barry, his son, asked him if he'd like to move in with him. In return, Barry insisted that his father transfer his home, small business, stocks, and other investments to him since it would all be left to him some day anyway. Jake agreed.

Within a year, Jake suffered a stroke, and while he suffered minimal loss of his mental faculties, he was partially paralyzed in his right side, necessitating assistance in getting dressed and moving around. Barry placed him in a nursing home as a pauper, where Jake was supported by Medicaid until he died a year later.

Discuss the following questions:

1. What types of violence or mistreatment are evident in this story?
2. What measures could have been taken to prevent the violence or mistreatment?

Jim and Mary's Story

Jim and Mary, married for thirty-eight years, had no children or close relatives. After Jim retired from a career as a electrician, he and Mary moved to a small rural community outside of town. Jim, age 69, was considerably overweight. He was more than twice Mary's weight and at least four inches taller. After six months in their new home, Jim suffered a heart attack, and his doctor ordered him to take it easy for three months.

About four months later, he developed pulmonary problems and grew weaker and weaker, necessitating that they purchase a hospital bed for him. During Jim's fourth month in bed, Mary and a neighbor were turning him onto his side and discovered a large bedsore on Bill's buttock. The neighbor insisted that Mary take Bill to the doctor immediately and perhaps either seek help in caring for Jim or even place Jim in a nursing home. Mary was adamant in believing that she could care for her husband by herself and that the bedsore would go away with the proper care she could give it.

Discuss the following questions:

1. What type of mistreatment is evident in this story?
2. What measures could have been taken to prevent the mistreatment?

Alice and Louise's Story

Alice, 54, and her mother, Louise, 77, began living together after Alice's husband divorced her. They shared household expenses equally and had ample money for vacations and visits to distantly located children and grandchildren. Alice took a part-time job at a local accounting firm. The job, her first since her first child was born thirty-four years earlier, became the center of her life. Soon her work and social life expanded to the point that she accepted full-time employment and began to spend several nights a week away from home with men she met through her work.

Alice's mother disapproved of her dating and was jealous of activities that took time Alice previously had devoted to mother-daughter shopping and travel. Alice no longer wanted to live with Louise but did not have the courage to say so. Instead, she began attempting to convince Louise that she was "senile" and belonged in a senior citizens' housing project.

After several months of listening to lectures about how forgetful and accident-prone she was, Alice's mother applied for an apartment at the senior citizens' center. By the time she was able to move to the center, her relationship with Alice was so seriously damaged that Alice did not visit her for more than six months. Largely due to her depressed condition and isolation, Louise became neglectful of her own well-being and was admitted to a hospital. She died seven months after she moved out of her daughter's home. None of the other children was told of the problem between Alice and Louise or of Louise's move until after she was in the hospital.[13]

Discuss the following questions:

1. What type of mistreatment is evident in this story?

2. What measures could have been taken to prevent the mistreatment?

Mrs. W.'s Story

Mrs. W., a widow, lived in a small townhouse in a large city. Her 50-year-old son, Fred, had lived in the family home all his life and like his father, who died at 56, became an alcoholic in early adulthood. Mrs. W., who was a diabetic and obese, had a substantial income from stocks, Social Security, and the rent that a small apartment in the building provided, and she never pressured her son to work.

Fred had little life of his own beyond drinking. As his small peer group became involved in their families and other interests, he became convinced that his life was ruined because of his mother's "hold" on him, but he made no effort to become independent. His mother excused his behavior, blaming it on his drinking.

When she was 84, Mrs. W. was hospitalized for fractures of the hip and lower jaw. Prior to this, she had been examined five times for fractures and bruises on the face and torso. All of these injuries had been attributed to falls or "clumsiness," but they were actually caused by her son hitting or pushing her, usually when he was drinking. During her hospitalization, Fred, who was cosigner on all of her bank accounts, withdrew most of her cash, sold all her stocks, and deposited these funds in new accounts in his own name. When Mrs. W. was discharged from the hospital, she found that her son had taken most of her assets and burned her furniture. He told her to "hurry up and die."

Mrs. W. lived for four more years as a prisoner in her own home. The case came to light when an acquaintance complained to a neighborhood [minister] that Mrs. W.'s son wouldn't let her out of the home. Mrs. W. was moved to a nursing home and died shortly after admission. An autopsy revealed that she had been beaten regularly and suffered multiple fractures up to the time that she was removed from the home. Without witnesses or evidence, no charges were brought against her son, who continued to live in the home.[14]

Discuss the following questions:

1. What types of violence or mistreatment are evident in this story?

2. What measures could have been taken to prevent the violence or mistreatment?

---

[13]*Domestic Mistreatment*, pp. 13–14.

[14]*Domestic Mistreatment*, p. 15.

Towards Prevention[15]

Towards Prevention . . . for Individuals

DOs

- Stay sociable as you age; maintain and increase your network of friends and acquaintances.
- Keep in contact with old friends and neighbors if you move in with a relative or change to a new address.
- Develop a "buddy system" with a friend outside the home. Plan for at least a weekly contact and share openly with this person.
- Ask friends to visit you at home; even a brief visit can allow observations of your well-being.
- Accept new opportunities for activities. They can bring new friends.
- Participate in community activities as long as you are able.
- Volunteer or become a member or officer of an organization. Participate regularly.
- Have your own telephone; post and open your own mail. If your mail is being intercepted, discuss the problem with postal authorities.
- Stay organized. Keep your belongings neat and orderly. Make sure others are aware that you know where everything is kept.
- Take care of your personal needs. Keep regular medical, dental, barber, hairdresser, and other personal appointments.
- Arrange to have your Social Security or pension check deposited directly to a bank account.
- Get legal advice about arrangements you can make now for possible future disability, including powers-of-attorney, guardianships, or conservatorships.
- Keep records, accounts, and property available for examination by someone you trust, as well as by the person you or the court has designated to manage your affairs.
- Review your will periodically.
- Give up control of your property or assets only when *you* decide you cannot manage them.
- Ask for help when you need it. Discuss your plans with your attorney, physician, or family members.

DON'Ts

- Don't live with a person who has a background of violent behavior or alcohol or drug abuse.
- Don't leave your home unattended. Notify police if you are going to be away for a long period. Don't leave messages on the door while you are away.
- Don't leave cash, jewelry, or prized possessions lying about.
- Don't accept personal care in return for transfer or assignments of your property or assets unless a lawyer, advocate, or another trusted person acts as a witness to the transaction.
- Don't sign a document unless someone you trust has reviewed it.
- Don't allow anyone else to keep details of your finances or property management from you.

---

[15]*Domestic Mistreatment*, pp. 2–5.

Towards Prevention . . . for Families

DOs

- Maintain close ties with aging relatives and friends. Keep abreast of changes in their health and ability to live independently.
- Discuss an older relative's wishes regarding health care, terminal medical care alternatives, home care in the case of incapacitation, and disposition of his or her personal assets.
- Find sources of help and *use* them. Chore services, housekeeping, home-delivered meals, senior recreation, day care, respite care, and transportation assistance are available in many communities.
- With the older person's consent, become familiar with his or her financial records, bank accounts, will, safe deposit boxes, insurance, debts, and sources of income before he or she becomes incapacitated. Talk and plan together *now* about how these affairs should be handled.
- Anticipate potential incapacitation by planning as a family who will take responsibility such as power-of-attorney or in-home caregiving if an aging relative becomes incapacitated.
- Closely examine your family's ability to provide long-term, in-home care for a frail and increasingly dependent relative. Consider the family's physical limits.
- Plan how your own needs will be met when your responsibility for the dependent older relative increases.
- Explore alternative sources of care, including nursing homes or other relatives' homes, in case your situation changes.
- Discuss your plans with friends, neighbors, and other sources of support before your responsibilities become a burden. Ask for their understanding and emotional support—you may need them.
- Familiarize family members with emergency response agencies and services available in case of sudden need.

DON'Ts

- Don't offer personal home care unless you thoroughly understand and can meet the responsibilities and costs involved.
- Don't wait until a frail older person has moved in with you to examine his or her needs. You'll need to consider access, safety, containment, and special needs. (Do you need a first-floor bathroom, bedroom, or entry ramp? Will carpets or stairs become barriers? Do you need a fenced yard to prevent the loved one from wandering away? Does your kitchen allow you to prepare special diets or store medications properly? Can you move the person safely in case of fire?)
- Don't assume that poor interpersonal relationships between you, or other members of the household, and the older person involved will disappear.
- Don't expect irritating habits or problems such as alcohol abuse to stop or be controlled once the dependent moves into your home.
- Don't ignore your limitations and overextend yourself. Passive neglect could result.
- Don't hamper the older person's independence or intrude unnecessarily upon his or her privacy. Provide a private telephone if you can and make other changes if possible.
- Don't label your efforts a failure if home care is not possible and you must seek an alternative.

Towards Prevention . . . for Communities

DOs

- Develop new ways to provide direct assistance to caregiving families. Improve crisis response to help families that face the difficult decision to discontinue home care.
- Through public awareness programs, advocate the cause of caregiving families and the needs of victims of mistreatment.
- Ask other community groups to become more involved in aging service programs, including those at nursing homes or senior citizen housing projects. Their involvement can lead to improved facilities and services.
- Encourage both public and private employers to help caregiving families, especially those with caregivers nearing or beyond retirement age, with fixed incomes and increasing health problems.
- Publicize available support services and professionals available to caregivers, such as senior day-care centers, chore services, companions, and housekeeping services. Caregivers may not know about them.
- Give public agency employees basic training in responses and case management. They can be trained to recognize some of the causes of neglect or abuse of older persons and can help in support roles.
- Provide training for community "gatekeepers" and service workers—primary care physicians, public health and social workers, law enforcement officers, transportation and utility workers, postal employees and others—to help them recognize at-risk situations and take appropriate action.
- Expand Neighborhood Watch programs and similar community groups to include training on home care of frail elderly, identification of the signs of mistreatment, and how to provide assistance or initiate preventive actions to reduce such victimization.
- Open your eyes and ears to the possibility that mistreatment is occurring. Become aware of individuals who are at risk. Develop procedures for investigation, public education, and public support of assistance to troubled families.
- Recognize that many forms of mistreatment or abuse are *crimes*. Volunteers can help victims file formal complaints, seek compensation for losses, seek prosecution of guilty parties, and give the victim assistance subsequent to prosecution. Prosecution can result in sentencing, diversion, training, counseling, or other types of family assistance services as alternatives to criminal sanctions. Urge public support of agencies to provide the necessary services.

DON'Ts

- Don't ignore family caregivers of dependent elderly. They are significant parts of the community. Community services can try to involve isolated people in appropriate services or self-help programs. Those at risk, living in isolation, may simply lack knowledge or information and may welcome community outreach.
- Don't assume that gerontology is a study confined to universities and hospitals. Begin to educate the entire community about aging. (This should be as common in public education as information about childcare.)
- Don't sensationalize stories of abuse of older persons. Instead, try to arouse public interest in techniques and strategies to prevent abuse.
- Don't start a major intervention just because an older person is alone or is said to be eccentric. The goal is to seek the least intrusive alternative.

Part 3

Worship Resources

O LORD, you will hear the desire of the meek;
    you will strengthen their heart,
        you will incline your ear
    to do justice for the orphan and the oppressed,
        so that those from earth may strike terror no more.
                                    —*Psalm 10:17–18*

A Day to Begin Healing Domestic Violence

Introduction

The committee (The Saskatchewan Conference's Human Development and Support Committee) that wrote this service believes that the church, in the past, has been part of the problem of domestic violence, especially male violence against women. In its support of patriarchy, in its glorification of certain Scriptures, the church has, if not explicitly, at least implicitly, supported those who abuse and encouraged acquiescence by those who are abused. The objective in this worship experience is to begin to change that pattern by owning [up to] the church's past complicity and by offering those who have been abused and those who abuse the opportunity to seek healing and transformation.

It is a fundamental assertion of this paper that God does not condone gender domination, nor the violence that acts to enforce it, nor can God's church. By taking a closer and careful look at the issues around Christian theology and practice, we believe that the church can become what it has not yet fully been—an agent to effect an end to the tragedy of abuse.

Statistical Background

There are many examples of violence in our society. This service is concerned with one aspect of family violence—violence by men directed against their partners. It is part of a larger pattern of oppression inherent in patriarchy: the tradition of male domination, condoned male privilege and violence in society, which exists today and has existed throughout the Christian era.

One million Canadian women are beaten every year by their male partners; that is, one in ten Canadian women report abuse (the actual statistics are believed to be much higher and do not include emotional and psychological abuse).

It takes an average of thirty-five beatings before a woman will call the police.

Only 5 percent of female victims of domestic abuse are described as such in medical records.

A recent U.S. study points out that 37 percent of women are physically abused during pregnancy; abuse is a leading cause of birth defects and infant mortality.

Misusing the Bible

We need to acknowledge that some Scripture is irredeemably patriarchal and misogynous. Some horrific examples from Scripture include the following:

Genesis 16: the Hagar study

2 Samuel 13:1–22: the rape of Tamar

Judges 19:1–30: the rape and murder of a concubine

Judges 11:29–30: the murder of Jephthah's daughter

These and similar texts that devalue women as chattel and sex objects cannot be uncritically proclaimed without contributing to the oppression of women. They need to be balanced with Scriptures that employ feminine images of God and that highlight the contributions of women.

Yet it is important to affirm that the Jewish and Christian Scriptures do not justify abuse in the family and are frequently misused.

Misuse and Flawed Theology Include:

- when suffering is seen as God's judgement or punishment for sin;
- when suffering is seen as abandonment by God;
- when mindless obedience and subservience, including acquiescence to violence, is seen as responding to the dictates of God;
- when preachers offer only simple words of advice for living that deny the reality of real suffering by reducing live experiences to simplistic slogans, such as if you are a good Christian, God will look after you;
- when preachers offer only the theology of the cross with no hope of resurrection, for example God expects suffering, even desires it. It is our lot and brings us closer to Christ. The church frequently uses the suffering servant songs as models of Christian virtue;
- when the needs and importance of maintaining the family are considered to be more important than ending abusive situations.

These notions are utterly contrary to the God of mercy, compassion, and liberation from the suffering and bondage, which is central to both the Hebrew and New Testament Scriptures alike. Suffering happens because of human sin, not because God wills it. God does not promise that we will not suffer, but does promise to be with us in our suffering, helping us to seek and find liberation. We are always called to choose life over death and that surely means that abuse must be confronted and ended. That is the liberation offered to the people of the exodus. We must never forget that the exodus journey was through a wilderness, but towards a promised land. That journey makes no sense without the resurrection to a new and better live.

The reassurance that God will not abandon us is very important to those who are abused. But just as important is the knowledge that God does not desire the suffering and seeks healing for both the abused and those who abuse. If this understanding is true, then God's church must never stand idly by when abuse is taking place, but always, and with great care, help people to find and choose life, that is, find a means of ending the abuse.

Pauline Literature

Christians have long misused Pauline literature (Ephesians, Colossians, and Corinthians) to try to justify abuse and patriarchy. But a closer look at the Scripture can give us a completely different picture. For example, Eph. 5:21 says: "Be subject to one another out of reverence for Christ." It is the first and most important verse about marriage, and it is often overlooked.

Later in 5:28–29 Paul writes: "Even so husbands should love their wives as their own bodies. He who loves his wife loves himself. For no man hates his own flesh but nourishes it and cherishes it, as Christ does the church because we are members of his body."

Battering is a clear and blatant violation of Scripture and reflects the self-hatred of the abuser. To condone or even seem to condone the violence is to do a terrible disservice to Scripture, the abused, and the abuser alike. There can be no complete healing without liberation for the one abused and repentance by the one who abuses.

Forgiveness and Transformation

Confession and forgiveness is another whole area of concern in dealing with abuse. We need, as the worshiping community, to assure the confessing abuser of God's forgiveness, but also to confront them with the need to pursue counseling or some other accountable work toward attitudinal and behavioral change. True repentance, after all, means transformation.

On the other hand, the one abused need not focus on forgiving the one who abuses or feel guilty for not being able to do so. Some form of forgiving of the abuser is needed for complete healing. But it is important that those who have been abused work at their own pace on forgiveness. It may take years, if ever, before they can finally forgive the abuser. In the meanwhile, it can be left to God to handle the forgiveness of the abuser. Forgiveness, for the victim, may mean simply the ability to get on with life and not allow the abuser of the past to dominate her or his life any more.

But forgiveness of self by the one abused is key and necessary—not forgiveness for having encouraged the abuser or any such perverted concept of forgiveness, but forgiveness for all the self-hatred that the abuser planted and nourished in the one abuse.

Breaking the Pattern

One important way to break the pattern is to accept our responsibility to reexamine our worship planning and preaching to ensure that we do not implicitly or explicitly endorse or condone family violence. On the contrary, we should name it as sin and condemn it as unacceptable and an affront to the God of peace, love, and justice that we are called to proclaim in our worship.

The church has a very long and tragic record of encouraging those who are abused to acquiesce and of supporting abusers in their expectation that they have a right to abuse. The question for the church today is, how are we going to break the chain of violence, especially the one that links patriarchy and misinterpretation of Scripture with the pattern of domestic violence?

Specifically, we need to reexamine and challenge the biblical messages that support the subordination of women and the theology that glorifies suffering as something redemptive and therefore pleasing to God.[1]

---

[1]Reprinted with permission from "Family Violence Awareness Sunday," published by the Fear Not Now Committee of the Pictou County Council of Churches, Nova Scotia, December 1996, pp. 33–35.

Sermon Themes[2]

Breaking the Silence of Abuse

As Christians we have often been reluctant to acknowledge that abuse happens in our homes and our churches. These Scriptures illustrate that God's people have always struggled with sexual and domestic violence. These biblical stories assist us in naming violence in our own lives.

Biblical Texts   Judges 11:29–40
                        2 Samuel 13:1–19
                        Psalm 55:1–15, 20–21
                        John 8:31–32

Suffering, Abandonment, Hope

These texts demonstrate the range of emotions that survivors may feel. The journey toward healing involves intense pain and intense feelings, including feelings of being abandoned by God. Caring church people can become a source of hope when they provide safe places for pain and a whole range of feelings to be expressed.

Biblical Texts   Psalm 22
                        Psalm 27
                        Isaiah 25:4–5
                        Romans 8:31–39

Church's Response to Survivors

Sometimes our tendency is to blame the "victim" for the abuse they have suffered. These passages demonstrate that Jesus honours peoples' pain and suffering. Jesus' healing power is demonstrated by his compassionate nonjudgmental response to suffering.

Biblical Texts   John 9:1–7
                        John 4:7–14
                        Luke 8:40–48
                        Luke 10:29–37

Church's Response to Perpetrators

Responding to perpetrators in our midst may be one of the most difficult challenges we face. Our tendency might be to avoid or to "shun" offenders. These biblical texts emphasize naming offenses as sin, holding offenders accountable for their actions, and challenging them to repent, to turn away from evil.

Biblical Texts   Matthew 18:15–18
                        Galatians 6:1–2

---

[2]*Lord, Hear Our Prayers: Domestic Violence Worship Resources*, compiled by Kathy Shantz. Published by Mennonite Central Committee Canada, 1994, p. 3. Used by permission.

Calls to Worship

God of compassion, you feel our pain and cry with us in our passion. God of justice, you rage with us against the injustice of our experience. Be with us today.

We gather today in sadness to remember all victims of violence, but especially those women and children who have been victims of violence in their own homes.

We come together because there is so much violence experienced every day by the vulnerable ones in our world: countless women, children, and men.[3]

Leader: We are gathered in the presence of God, who asks us to choose between life and death, blessing and cursing.

People: We are gathered like the people of Israel, who were challenged to choose the way of life.

Leader: Like them, we often follow the ways of death.

People: Yet, like them, we have the freedom each day to begin anew by the grace of God.

Leader: By our presence here, we are saying that we want to choose life one more time.

All: Let us praise the God of love and life who has called us to this place. Amen.[4]

Come to Christ, the living bread, who satisfies those who hunger and thirst for what is right. Come to Christ, who gives living water, that you may never thirst again.

Come to Christ, that being filled yourself, you may minister to the hunger and thirst of others. Come to God, in worship and praise, through Jesus Christ, who gives us life.[5]

We gather today to worship a living God, a God who hears our cries, shares our tears, knows our anger, and is steadfast now and always.

We gather today to be in each other's presence as we remember, confess, name, and respond to the violence in our lives, in our families, our churches and our communities.

Let us walk this way together.[6]

---

[3]*Lord, Hear Our Prayers*, p. 3.

[4]*Bread for the Journey*, ed. Ruth C. Duck, 1981. Reprinted with the permission of The Pilgrim Press.

[5]*Touch Holiness*, ed. Ruth C. Duck and Maren C. Tirabassi, 1990. Reprinted with the permission of The Pilgrim Press.

[6]*Leader's Guide: World Community Day for November 1, 1996*. NY: Church Women United, 475 Riverside Drive, Room 812. New York, NY 10115, p. 4.

One: Come, all who are weary and heavy-laden; come, all who seek God's rest and peace.

People: We come with reluctance, knowing the pain and suffering and fear of our lives, fearing that they may be revealed.

One: Come before our God, who knows the hidden depths of each heart, and knowing, loves us completely.

People: We come with expectation, seeking out of our confusion and fear the light and hope of God's love.

One: Come, all who seek transformation. Let us worship our God who offers us new life.[7]

Invitation to Confession

Dear Friends, God knows and understands the heart of each one of us. In that understanding, God reaches out lovingly to call us to repent of all our wrongdoing and to seek new ways of living with one another. When we confess our sins as a community, we do not usually separate anyone from the whole body, but make our confession as one unit. Today, however, we want to be especially sensitive to the fact that the body of Christ is divided, for some are abused, some are abusers, and some condone the abuse by looking away. As the community of faith, let us join with God and with one another in making our confession before God.

A Litany of Confession

All: God of wisdom and mercy, you have created a world of beauty, a world where each one has a special and honoured place in your love. Forgive us that some of us have not honoured one another as you have honoured each of us. O God, in your mercy, forgive us.

One: O God, for all the times when some of us have not valued ourselves as people created in your image . . .

People: O God, in your mercy, forgive us.

One: O God, for all the times when we have known of the suffering of others but turned away from it . . .

People: O God, in your mercy, forgive us.

One: O God, for all the times when some of us have seen pain and blamed it on those who suffer . . .

People: O God, in your mercy, forgive us.

One: O God, for all the times when some of us have cried out in pain but blamed ourselves, for the times when we burdened ourselves with guilt when we suffered injustice at another's hand . . .

People: O God, in your mercy, help us, befriend us, hear our cry, comfort us, send us a friend, let someone see. . . .

---

[7]"Family Ministries and Seniors," Saskatchewan Conference Human Development and Support Committee, Volume 8, Spring 1993. Used by permission.

One: O God, for all the times when some of us have heard cries of pain and not believed them . . .

People: O God, in your mercy, forgive us.

One: O God, for all the times when we alone, or as a church, have not sought to end pain and bring about your justice . . .

People: O God, in your mercy, forgive us.

One: O God, for all the times when we ourselves have been the cause of human suffering . . .

People: O God, in your mercy, forgive us.

One: Loving God, you alone know how these burdens weigh on our souls. Forgive us, free us, and show us the paths of love you would have us choose. Amen.[8]

A Litany of Confession

Leader: Every 15 seconds a woman in the U.S. is subjected to violent abuse at the hand of her spouse or intimate partner for a total of 4–6 million reported incidents per year.

All: *"There is a balm is Gilead to make the wounded whole, there is a balm in Gilead to heal the sin-sick soul."*

Leader: Thirty-five to forty percent of battered women attempt suicide. Wife abuse accounts for 25 percent of suicides by all U.S. women and 50 percent of suicides by African American women.

All: *"There is a balm is Gilead to make the wounded whole, there is a balm in Gilead to heal the sin-sick soul."*

Leader: One in five women is raped in her lifetime. Seventy-eight percent of rapes are committed by relatives, friends, or neighbors.

All: *"There is a balm is Gilead to make the wounded whole, there is a balm in Gilead to heal the sin-sick soul."*

Leader: Eighty-four to ninety percent of child sexual abuse cases are never reported to law enforcement or protective services agencies. In over 80 percent of reported cases, the perpetrator is someone known to the family.

All: *"There is a balm is Gilead to make the wounded whole, there is a balm in Gilead to heal the sin-sick soul."*

Leader: Over 1,000,000 older adults are physically, financially, and emotionally abused by relatives or loved ones annually.

All: *"There is a balm is Gilead to make the wounded whole, there is a balm in Gilead to heal the sin-sick soul."*

Leader: The likelihood of a case [of elder abuse] being reported depends on state laws, local police practices, Social Services assistance levels, court-related activities, and the people involved. . . . One thing is certain: the vast majority of cases in all likelihood don't come to public attention.

---

[8]"Family Ministries and Seniors," p. 35.

All: *"There is a balm is Gilead to make the wounded whole, there is a balm in Gilead to heal the sin-sick soul."*

Leader: Disabled children are two to three times more likely than their nondisabled peers to be sexually abused.

All: *"There is a balm is Gilead to make the wounded whole, there is a balm in Gilead to heal the sin-sick soul."*

Leader: One child is killed each day in the U.S. by a family member, and 90 percent of these children are under five. Half of the children killed are infants in homes where their mothers are being battered. Children themselves are at great risk for abuse and serious neglect.

All: *"There is a balm is Gilead to make the wounded whole, there is a balm in Gilead to heal the sin-sick soul."*

Sources: *Elder Abuse: A National Disgrace*, House Select Committee on Aging, 1981; *Domestic Mistreatment of the Elderly—Towards Prevention*, AARP, 1992; *Counterpoint*, National Association of State Directors of Special Education, Vol 12, No 3, Spring 1992; *Myths and Realities about Child Sexual Abuse*, by Carol E. Jordan, MS; Sexual and Domestic Violence Administrator, Department of Mental Health and Mental Retardation Services; *Laws against Sexual and Domestic Violence: A Concise Guide for Clergy and Laity*, NY: Pilgrim Press, 1988, p. 2, and the NCPCA, 1991.

Prayers of Confession

O God, You know our hearts, our minds, our feelings, and our thoughts. You know the heavy stones that weigh down our spirits. We cry for all that cannot be saved. Comfort us as we mourn the loss of women's lives to violence. Strengthen us as we break the silence, confront evil, and cry out for justice. Help us see the chains that bind us and the chains that we place around others. Set us free to walk in the fullness of life that is promised to all people. Let us live into that promise with every moment of our lives. Amen.[9]

O merciful one, we confess that by our silence and inaction we have passed by on the other side, leaving a sister suffering by the side of the road. We confess that in our fear, we have hesitated and turned away from life, adding to the pain and suffering.

Bring us to repentance.

O Holy one,

Open our eyes to see the violence in our lives, within us and among us.

Open our mouths to name what we see and to acknowledge our own pain.

Open our hearts to let in the pain and suffering of family members, friends, child victims, adult survivors, and our neighbors.

Open our mouths to call to account those who have harmed others.

Be merciful and bring us back to life in Christ. Amen.[10]

---

[9]*Leader's Guide: World Community Day*, p. 6.

[10]*Leader's Guide: World Community Day*, p. 17–18.

Assurance of Pardon

Sisters and brothers, hear the good news! There is no sin so large, no shortcoming so great that it can separate us from the love of God. For all who truly desire new life, God offers forgiveness and new opportunities for healing and wholeness in our lives. Accept God's grace and live![11]

Prayers of People

Prayer of Dedication

We offer ourselves to you, O God our Creator. We offer our hands.

Use healing touch to comfort sisters, brothers, and children who are afraid.

We offer our eyes and ears. May we see and hear the signs and stories of violence so that all may have someone with them in their pain and confusion.

We offer our hearts and our tears as their hurt and sorrow echo within us.

We offer our own stories of violence.

May we be healed as we embrace each other.

We offer our anger. Make it a passion for justice.

We offer all our skills. Use our gifts to end violence.

We offer our faith, our hope, our love. May our encounters with violence bring us closer to you and to each other.

All this we ask through Jesus Christ who knows the pain of violence. Amen.[12]

God of Love and Justice

God of love and justice,

we long for peace within and peace without.

We long for harmony in our families,

for serenity in the midst of struggle.

We long for the day when our homes

will be a dwelling place for your love.

Yet we confess that we are often anxious;

we do not trust each other,

and we harbour violence.

We are not willing to take the risks

and make the sacrifices that love requires.

Look upon us with kindness and grace.

Rule in our homes and in all the world;

show us how to walk in your paths,

through the mercy of our Saviour. Amen.[13]

---

[11]"Family Ministries and Seniors," pp. 35–36.

[12]Excerpted from the 1992 Women's Interchurch Council of Canada *Worship Service* in remembrance of the December 6, 1989, massacre of 14 women in Montreal.

[13]*Lord, Hear Our Prayers*, p. 21.

God of Peace and Comfort

God of peace and comfort,

we pray for those who are not safe in their own homes

or with people they care about because of domestic violence.

Give strength and courage to those who are abused and battered.

Grant repentance to those who abuse the ones they love.

Help all of us to nurture one another in the spirit of love and peace proclaimed

by Jesus Christ,

in whose name we pray. Amen. [14]

Charges and Benedictions

Now, go and breathe deeply, for each breath is from God;

go and serve gently, for the earth and its people are fragile;

go with energy and strength, for God knows your every need, and God's

Spirit will grant you peace. [15]

Stay with us, O God,

for the day is far spent

and we have not yet recognized Your face

in each of our brothers and sisters.

> Stay with us, O God,
>
> for the day is far spent
>
> and we have not yet shared Your bread
>
> in grace with our bothers and sisters.

Stay with us, O God,

for the day is far spent

and we have not listened to Your Word

in the words of our brothers and sisters.

> Stay with us, O God,
>
> for the day is far spent
>
> and our hearts are still so slow to believe
>
> that you had to die in order to rise again.

Stay with us, O God,

because our very night becomes day

when you are there. [16]

---

[14]Sharon K. Youngs, *Confronting Domestic Violence: Not Just for Adults.* Louisville: Curriculum Publishing, Presbyterian Church (U.S.A.), 1996, p. 6.

[15]*Peacemaking Through Worship*, Volume 2, Ed. Jane Parker Huber. Presbyterian Peacemaking Program of the Presbyterian Church (U.S.A.), 1992, p. 126. Used by permission.

[16]*Peacemaking Through Worship*, p. 127.

Litanies

Let Love Be Genuine

Group One: Society says, "Don't worry about taking advantage of others."

Group Two: But the Scripture says, "Let love be genuine."

Group One: Our culture says, "Being male is an asset; being female is a liability."

Group Two: But the Scripture says, "Hate what is evil, hold fast to what is good."

Group One: Society says, "Look out for Number One."

Group Two: But the Scripture says, "Love one another with mutual affection."

Group One: Our culture says, "Turn your head the other way; someone else will eventually help."

Group Two: But the Scripture says, "Outdo one another in showing honor."

All: O God, open our ears to hear clearly your words of Scripture. Give us a strong resolve to live our lives as the people you desire us to be— people of loving and peace-filled ways.

(Litany based on Rom. 12:9–10)[17]

A Litany of Courage

Leader: Paul writes, "So then, putting away falsehood, let all of us speak the truth to our neighbors." O God in whom there is no falsehood, teach us how to express our feelings in healthy ways. Help us to find our voices to name and confront domestic violence, especially when it is happening to those we know—or even to ourselves. With boldness we pray,

All: Give us courage to speak the truth, O God.

Leader: Paul writes that we are members of one another. O God of community, help us to remember that we are not alone. Thank you for the persons in our lives with whom we can share our joys as well as our pains. With boldness we pray,

All: Give us courage to speak the truth, O God.

Leader: Paul writes, "Be angry but do not sin; do not let the sun go down on your anger." O Source of Justice, help us to remember that you—not we—are God. Show us how to live in right relationship with all of your children. Grant that we may never take for granted those about whom we care the most. With boldness we pray,

All: Give us courage to speak the truth, O God.

Leader: So be it. Go in peace and safety.[18]

---

[17]*Confronting Domestic Violence*, p. 13.

[18]*Confronting Domestic Violence*, p. 21.

Remembering

Leader 1: O God of compassion, you feel our pain and cry with us in our passion.

All: God of justice, you rage with us against the injustice of our experiences of violence and abuse. Be with us today.

Leader 1: As sisters of faith and hope, gathered here today, we remember:

Left Side: Our mothers, who had few choices; who did what they had to; who resisted sometimes quietly, sometimes loudly; who carried the secrets of their abuse silently in their hearts.

Right Side: Our sisters, who were made the scapegoat; who said, "No!" but to no avail; who thought they were protecting us; who were given tranquilizers to quiet their rage; who carried the secrets of their abuse silently in their hearts.

Left Side: Our neighbors, whose cries we heard in the night, whose bruises we saw in the day, who fought back and paid the price, who carried the secret of their abuse silently in their hearts.

Right Side: Our girlfriends, who spent so much time at our house, not wanting to go home; whom everyone thought were just shy and quiet; who carried the secrets of their abuse silently in their hearts.

Left Side: Ourselves, who may have tried to tell but were ignored; who were not protected by anyone; who were not believed; who carry the secrets of our abuse silently in our hearts.

Right Side: We remember and mourn the loss of childhood; the loss of creativity; the loss of vocation; the loss of relationships; the loss of time; the cost of resources required for healing; the enormous waste of humanity caused by sexual and domestic violence.

All: We remember and mourn those who have not survived; whose lives were taken by someone's violence; who died in despair never knowing justice.[19]

---

[19]*Leader's Guide: World Community Day for Nov. 1, 1996.* Church Women United, 475 Riverside Drive, Room 812, New York, NY 10115.

There Is a Balm in Gilead

Is there no balm in Gilead? Is there no physician there? Jer. 8:22

(Ref.) There is a balm in Gil - e - ad to make the wound - ed whole,
there is a balm in Gil - e - ad to heal the sin - sick soul.

1. Some - times I feel dis - cour - aged, and think my work's in vain,
2. If you can - not preach like Pe - ter, if you can - not pray like Paul,
3. Don't ev - er feel dis - cour - aged, for Je - sus is your friend

but then the Ho - ly Spir - it re - vives my soul a - gain.
you can tell the love of Je - sus, and say, "He died for all."
and if you lack for knowl - edge he'll ne'er re - fuse to lend.

Words and Music: Afro-American Spiritual

Open My Eyes That I May See

OPEN MY EYES   8.8.9.8 with refrain

Clara H. Scott, 1895   Clara H. Scott, 1895

1. O - pen my eyes, that I may see   Glimps - es of truth Thou hast for me;
2. O - pen my ears, that I may hear   Voic - es of truth Thou send - est clear;
3. O - pen my mouth, and let me bear   Glad - ly the warm truth ev - ery - where;

Place in my hands the won - der - ful key   That shall un - clasp and set me free.
And while the wave notes fall on my ear,   Ev - ery - thing false will dis - ap - pear.
O - pen my heart, and let me pre - pare   Love with Thy chil - dren thus to share.

Refrain

Si - lent - ly now I wait for Thee,   Read - y, my God, Thy will to see;

O - pen my   eyes,
          ears, il - lu - mine me,   Spir - it di - vine!
          heart,

Appendix A

A Model for Child Abuse Prevention Education: Volunteer and Staff Training in the Church

Developed by Susan Keil Smith, member of the Presbyterian Child Advocacy Network

The Presbyterian Church (U.S.A.) has a rich history of ministry to children and youth. Our church has always stressed the sanctity of human life and the importance and worth of each individual as a child of God. It is our call and spiritual mandate to protect those entrusted to our care. As the church of Jesus Christ, we are committed to protecting the children and are bound by God to intervene on behalf of any child we believe is being harmed.

The following is an outline of a model about child safety issues, expanding our ministries, and protecting children from abuse and harm. It is also about heightening our awareness of signs of abuse and neglect, what to do if we suspect abuse, which church policies and procedures exist regarding work with children, and what are developmentally appropriate methods for teaching and disciplining.

If I were seeking a quality care weekday situation for my child, I would insist on the very best circumstance. Why should I not do the same for programs at my church? We must create a safe environment for children in our churches. We must be realistic about expectations for quality care and specifically address the legalistic society in which we live. We must think proactively about what must be done to keep God's children safe.

The following plan can be implemented in a three-hour session and used with paid church staff, as well as volunteers. The critical information is the same, but the application and screening process may differ in that fully employed persons might be requested to complete additional requirements appropriate to their roles.

1. Explain why the church provides this opportunity for awareness training. (10 minutes)
   a. The statistics show that in America, every 47 seconds a child is abused, and every day 3 children die from child abuse, 15 children die from guns, and 8,189 children are reported abused or neglected (statistics from the Children's Defense Fund).
   b. Children's ministry is a sacred responsibility.
   c. Keeping children safe is a high priority.
   d. Workers are accountable and must use good judgment.
   e. The moral tone of our society insists that we address legalistic issues in a responsible way.
   f. The National Child Protection Act of 1993 addresses screening of paid workers as well as volunteers who work with children. (See the full Act in Appendix B, pp. 112–116.)
2. Present the goals for this training. (5 minutes)
   The goals of this training include helping the congregation to

   - develop an awareness of child abuse, its prevalence, and its impact on the lives of children, parents, and the congregation
   - explore how Christian faith provides support for our commitment to keeping children safe

- understand the barriers to developing child abuse prevention programs and policy within the congregation
- become acquainted with prevention programs available for churches
- equip participants to respond effectively when child abuse occurs

It is hoped that, by the end of the training, participants will be able to

- explain to others what child sexual abuse is and how it affects the community of believers
- articulate for themselves a sense of how their faith calls them to address child abuse concerns
- list the common reasons why churches have not been active in preventing child sexual abuse
- develop strategies for overcoming these barriers
- know how to respond to a report of child sexual abuse
- list and understand important factors to be included in church policies and procedures addressing abuse concerns

3. Discuss the church's involvement in child advocacy. (10 minutes)

Review the following documents of our denomination and passages from God's Word:

a. The Confession of 1967: In baptism, the church celebrates the renewal of the covenant. (See p. 110.)

b. *The Book of Order:* The congregation as a whole, on behalf of the Church universal, assumes responsibility for nurturing the baptized person in the Christian life (W-2.3013). (See p. 110.)

c. General Assembly statements, 1991, 1996. (See p. 111.)

d. Scripture basis for child advocacy:

Deut. 30:19, choose life

Prov. 13:24, those who spare the rod . . .

Mal. 4:6, turning hearts of parents to their children

Mark 9:36–37, welcoming the children

Mark 10:13–16, Jesus blessing the children

Luke 17:1–3, forgiveness? the dilemma

1 Cor. 3:16–17, Our bodies are God's holy temple; we are called to be advocates for the victims.

In 1992, the Presbyterian Child Advocacy Network (PCAN) became a network of the Presbyterian Health, Education, and Welfare Association, with bylaws, goals, and budget. The purpose of PCAN includes supporting "the development and implementation of public and private policies for the needs and rights of all children as outlined in the United Nations Convention on the Rights of the Child." For more information, call the Presbyterian Child Advocacy Office at 1-502-569-5838.

4. View *Hear Their Cries.* (45 minutes)

This video is intended to raise awareness among clergy and lay people of the vulnerability of children and the need to intervene on their behalf. Child advocacy is a multifaceted, urgent issue. Sensitive areas such as child abuse, as well as the need for financial assistance, medical care, and breaking the poverty cycle, involve adults as well as children. It is our moral obligation as Christians to be aware of the needs of all children.

Child abuse is an emotionally charged topic. This video stresses important points, such as what child abuse and child neglect are, recognizing signs of neglect, and what should be done if child abuse is suspected.

These questions must be well addressed in a faith context. Clergy, lay people, and victims share their experiences in this compelling interdenominational piece.

5. Discuss *Hear Their Cries*. (30 minutes)

Using the study guide, discuss the questions raised in the video (Note: Leader must view this video prior to showing it to a group). If possible, have a trained social services professional guide this section and the next.

6. Discuss what we need to know about child sexual abuse. (15 minutes)

   a. Summarize the important points from "Who Abuses a Child?" on pp. 38–40.

   b. Review the "Behavioral Indicators of Child Sexual Abuse" found on p. 43.

   c. Make it clear that if there is evidence of possible child abuse, any investigation must have a professionally trained person in the room. Investigations should not be instigated by people who are not professionally trained in the best and most helpful way to obtain information.

7. Discuss the church's response to and prevention of child sexual abuse. (20 minutes)

Review the following steps and discuss in concrete ways how the church could respond to, address, and prevent sexual abuse.

   (1) If abuse is suspected:

   • Observe signs. (See p. 43)

   • Contact a paid professional member of staff.

   • Report to secular authorities.

   • Make it clear that all information is absolutely confidential. The seriousness of any child abuse situation necessitates that confidentiality be honored for all parties involved.

   (2) Emphasize the importance of having a criminal background check on all paid staff applicants, including a signed affidavit.

   (3) Develop a policy for screening volunteers. (See sample policy on pp. 108–110 and sample application form on pp. 106–107.)

8. View *Reducing the Risk*. (25 minutes)

This video in two parts is insurance driven but emphasizes the urgency of congregational involvement in abuse prevention education and the necessity to become involved. Consider showing this to the church session.

9. Review safety procedures. (15 minutes)

   a. Two-person rule: Two adults should be present during any church activity.

   b. Six-month rule: All persons who are working as volunteers with children and youth should be church members for at least six months.

c. Documentation of incidents and report to paid staff (see p. 105).

d. Critical nature of training: Reemphasize the importance of training staff and volunteers in recognizing the signs and symptoms of abuse and what steps need to be taken if abuse is suspected (see p. 103).

e. Knowing the families, pick-up procedures, identifying information: Emphasize the need for staff to know the family members of each child, the routine pick-up procedures, and ways to identify any person picking up the child if it is not a normal pick up.

Note: When using this model for volunteer training, conclude with the volunteer application, urging prospective volunteers to complete it immediately and thoughtfully.

Incident Report Form

Reason for report:_____

Date of Incident:_____ Time: _____

Name of Reporter:_____ Class:_____

Title:_____

Name(s) of Child(ren):_____ Ages(s): _____

Briefly describe what happened: _____
_____
_____
_____
_____
_____

What action did you take? _____
_____
_____
_____
_____
_____

Has the incident been resolved?___yes ___no   Explain: _____
_____
_____
_____
_____
_____

Were there any witnesses?___yes ___no

Names: _____
_____
_____
_____
_____
_____

Signatures (if possible): _____
_____
_____
_____

Report submitted to: _____

_____ **Church**

Adult Volunteer Application

General Information

Name_____ Date _____

Address _____

Phone (h)_____ (w) _____

List all other names you have been known by.

_____

_____

List three personal references we can contact on your behalf (not former employers or relatives).

1. Name _____
   Address _____
   City, State, Zip_____
   Telephone _____
2. Name _____
   Address _____
   City, State, Zip_____
   Telephone _____
3. Name _____
   Address _____
   City, State, Zip_____
   Telephone _____

In caring for children, we believe it is our responsibility to seek adult staff that is able to provide healthy, safe, and nurturing relationships. Please answer the following questions accordingly. Answering yes to any of the questions 3 through 5 will not automatically disqualify a volunteer from working with children. Any special concerns can be discussed individually with the pastoral staff.

1. Do you have a current driver's license? ___yes ___no
   If yes, please list your driver's license number _____
   (staff needs to make a photocopy of the driver's license)
2. Are you willing to be fingerprinted for a criminal records check? ___yes ___no
3. Have you ever been convicted of or pled guilty to a crime? ___yes ___no
   If yes, please describe: _____
   _____
   _____
   _____
4. Have you ever been a victim of any form of child abuse? ___ yes ___no
   If you prefer, you may discuss your answer in confidence with a pastor rather than answering it on this form.
5. Have you ever been in treatment for drug or alcohol abuse? ___yes ___no
   If yes, please explain: _____

_____

_____

_____

6. Are you using illegal drugs? ___yes ___no

The information contained in this application is correct to the best of my knowledge. I, the undersigned, authorize any references or churches listed in this application to release any and all records or information related to working with minors. The church staff at _____ Church may contact my references and appropriate government agencies as deemed necessary in order to verify my suitability as a (teacher, educator, caregiver . . .).

I understand that the personal information provided in this application will be held in strict confidentiality.

_____   _____

Signature   Date

Policy for the Screening of Volunteers

As an organization committed to developing strategies for the prevention of child abuse in the church, the session of _____ Church is determined that any and all adults who work on behalf of _____ Church with any youth will be properly selected, screened, trained, and supervised to minimize the risk of child abuse at _____ Church by volunteers or employees. For the purposes of this policy, youth is defined to mean anyone under the age of eighteen and/or any adult who is developmentally disabled.

Worker Selection

All persons who volunteer to work with youth in any capacity related to the work of _____ Church will be a member of this church for a period of at least six months.

All prospective volunteers who will be working with youth shall complete an application. The application will ask about prior volunteer or paid work with youth. It will ask for the names, addresses, and telephone numbers of three (3) references who are acquainted with the applicant's work with children and youth. Volunteers will also be asked about any prior accusations, arrests, or convictions for physical or sexual child abuse or neglect, child exploitation, or sexual misconduct in any capacity. There will be a request for permission to complete a criminal background check with the Department of Public Safety. *No one with known prior incidents of physical or sexual child abuse, child neglect, child exploitation, or other forms of sexual misconduct will be utilized in any capacity in contact with youth.*

No person shall be accepted for volunteer work with youth until *after* the application has been reviewed and approved and references have been checked.

Supervision

At least two adult workers shall be present at all activities sponsored by _____ Church involving children or youth. At no time shall only one worker be allowed to be alone with children or youth. The only exception to this two-adult policy would be in a situation in which the contact occurs in a public place and other persons are in and out of the area where the adult is working with youth.

All volunteers who work with children or youth will be trained in understanding the nature of child abuse and its effects on the lives of children, in recognizing signs of possible abuse, and in the reporting requirements of the state. Training will involve a one- to two-hour session, twice each year, in which the following topics will be covered:

- what constitutes child abuse
- recognizing signs and symptoms of child abuse
- state law concerning reporting
- _____ Church policy
- the importance of active listening and providing support
- the importance of volunteers *not* investigating allegations of abuse (of not asking questions of the alleged victim or the alleged perpetrator)
- explanation of the volunteer application and the importance of its completion

Reporting Abuse

If a volunteer has any knowledge or suspicion that abuse has occurred, he or she will report it immediately to the director of Christian education, youth coordinator, or senior minister. The volunteer and staff member will then make a confidential report to Child Protective Services. *It is imperative that volunteers not engage in questioning the alleged victim.*

The report shall contain information about

- the identity of the person(s) who are reporting the suspected abuse and where they can be located if further information is needed
- the identity of the child or youth who is the suspected victim and information about where he or she can be located for interview by CPS (home address, school, etc.)
- the identity of the alleged perpetrator and information about where he or she can be located
- the nature of the alleged abuse, injuries, and statements made by the alleged victim

A record will be kept in a designated confidential space that a report of suspected abuse or neglect was made. This notation will include the name of the agency and the staff person to whom the report was made, the date and time that the report was made, and the names of the persons making that report. Nothing confidential will be included in this notation.

Staff and Volunteer Training

It is vitally important that staff and volunteers be trained to recognize the signs and symptoms of abuse. This way intervention will happen when abuse is occurring, ensuring that the abuse stops and that those involved get the help they need. Children who are believed, protected, and helped when abuse is discovered are far less likely to have long-term problems or to become abusers themselves.

Training should include information on how to report, what to report, and to whom a report must be made. Consulting the Children's Code of your state will be important in providing this information. It also needs to be stressed that questioning the child for details is not the role of the staff or the volunteer. Too many people asking personal details about a difficult situation can increase the trauma to the child. It can also result in the child's story being questioned as having been influenced by leading questions (questions which suggest the expected answer) of persons not trained to do such an investigation. Investigations need to be left to the appropriate agency, whether it is child protective services or the police. The importance of confidentiality should also be addressed.

Staff and volunteers may also benefit from training on how to listen empathetically and to be supportive to child victims and their family. It may be helpful for them to understand the common symptoms and behavior changes that may occur after abuse so that they can help the child and parents understand that this is a normal response to abuse. Knowing when it is important to refer families for professional help may also be helpful. Understanding what happens after a report has been made will help staff and volunteers, as well as victims and their families, to feel more empowered and less frustrated by the delays that are sure to occur. It also allows the staff and volunteers who choose to do so to advocate for the child during the legal process.

Parents of victims often have great difficulty when learning about the abuse. They generally feel a great deal of guilt at not having known and not having been able to protect their child. Knowing the common emotional and behavioral responses of parents allows staff and volunteers to minister to their needs. This may be an important ministry to the child as well so that the parents' grief reactions don't interfere with the child getting their needs met.

Some of this training can be shared with parents and other members of the congregation so that they can be responsive to the needs of the victim(s), parents, and others involved. Much information can be disseminated through adult classes, discussion groups, bulletin inserts, resources in the church library, and even sermons.

It may also be important to understand how perpetrators often react to being discovered and appropriate responses by the church to these behaviors. While it is tempting to forgive and move on, it is essential that the perpetrator be held accountable, be expected to take responsibility (and to express that to the victim, if the victim is willing), and to make the change necessary to minimize the risk of their future involvement in child sexual abuse. The congregation may need help in dealing with not knowing for some time whether the accused is or is not guilty. Clearly, a person accused of sexually abusing children needs Christian love and support. However, this should never be at the expense of the safety of children.

The congregation itself will have some needs, and helping them to understand how the abuse could have occurred in their church and how to deal with their feelings will be an important ministry. It may be helpful in this to utilize outside resources so that staff accept this help and are not asked to minister to others when they are experiencing pain.

The Church Speaks

From The Confession of 1967

God has created the peoples of the earth to be one universal family. . . . (9.44)

. . . Reconciled to God, each person has joy in and respect for his [or her] own humanity and that of others persons; . . . parents receive the grace to care for children in love and to nurture their individuality. . . . (9.47)

. . . In baptism, the church celebrates the renewal of the covenant with which God has bound [God's] people. . . . By baptism, individuals are publicly received into the church to share in its life and ministry, and the church becomes responsible for their training and support in Christian discipleship. When those baptized are infants, the congregation, as well as the parents, has a special obligation to nurture them in the Christian life, leading them to make, by a public profession, a personal response to the love of God shown forth in their baptism. (9.51)

From the *Book of Order*

Both believers and their children are included in God's covenant love. . . . The Baptism of children witnesses to the truth that God's love claims people before they are able to respond in faith. (W–2.3008)

The congregation as a whole, on behalf of the Church universal, assumes responsibility for nurturing the baptized person in the Christian life. (W–2.3013)

From the Presbyterian Church (U.S.A.)
General Assembly Statement on Child Advocacy, 1991

. . . Whereas, the *Book of Order*, G–1.0200, states, "The great ends of the Church are the proclamation of the gospel for the salvation of humankind; the shelter, nurture, and spiritual fellowship of the children of God; the maintenance of divine worship; the preservation of the truth, the promotion of social righteousness; and the exhibition of the Kingdom of Heaven to the world"; and

Whereas, the *Book of Order* also states in W–2.3013, "The congregation as a whole, on behalf of the Church universal, assumes responsibility for nurturing the baptized person in the Christian life," and Presbyterians believe this baptismal commitment to be a serious one, understanding it to apply to all God's children; . . .

Therefore, the 203rd General Assembly (1991):

. . . Directs the agencies of the General Assembly and the governing bodies and congregations of the Presbyterian Church (U.S.A.) to develop clear strategies and specific programs to defend and improve the status of children and to address their current critical needs in education, nutrition, health care, housing, and security from abuse and exploitation.

. . . Urges every congregation to make the needs and rights of children and families a priority for life and mission in the 1990s.

. . . Calls on the church and its members at all levels to advocate and support the development and implementation of public and private policies for the needs and rights of children, built on a prevention/investment strategy aimed at meeting the needs of all children and families for adequate health care, . . . adequate and safe housing, quality child care and education, and protection from abuse and exploitation. . . .

From The Presbyterian Church (U.S.A.)
General Assembly Statement on the
Needs of Infants, Children, and Young People, 1996

Whereas, Jesus clearly underscored the value and importance of children; and

Whereas, children the world over continue to be undervalued, neglected, and abused; and

Whereas, the future of the church rests with our children and young people; . . .

Therefore, the 208th General Assembly (1996) of the Presbyterian Church (U.S.A.):

1. Refocuses its attention so that it is more intentional in dealing with the physical, affectional, emotional, spiritual, intellectual, and communal needs of infants, children, and young people.

2. Strongly urges each entity within the Presbyterian Church (U.S.A.) to seek appropriate ways to participate thoughtfully and enthusiastically in this effort.

Appendix B

Public Law 103-209 {H.R. 1237}; Dec. 20, 1993

NATIONAL CHILD PROTECTION ACT OF 1993

An Act to establish procedures for national criminal background checks for child care providers.
Be it enacted by the Senate and House of Representatives of the United States of America in Congress assembled,

SECTION 1. SHORT TITLE.

This Act may be cited as the "National Child Protection Act of 1993".

SEC 2. REPORTING CHILD ABUSE CRIME INFORMATION.

(a) IN GENERAL.—In each State, an authorized criminal justice agency of the State shall report child abuse crime information to, or index child abuse crime information in, the national criminal history background check system.

(b) PROVISION OF STATE CHILD ABUSE CRIME RECORDS THROUGH THE NATIONAL CRIMINAL HISTORY BACKGROUND CHECK SYSTEM.—(1) Not later than 180 days after the date of enactment of this Act, the Attorney General shall, subject to availability of appropriations—

(A) investigate the criminal history records system of each State and determine for each State a timetable by which the State should be able to provide child abuse crime records on an on-line basis through the national criminal history background check system;

(B) in consultation with State officials, establish guidelines for the reporting or indexing of child abuse crime information, including guidelines relating to the format, content, and accuracy of criminal history records and other procedures for carrying out this Act; and

(C) notify each State of the determinations made pursuant to subparagraphs (A) and (B).

(2) The Attorney General shall require as a part of each State timetable that the State—

(A) by not later than the date that is 3 years after the date of enactment of this Act, have in a computerized criminal history file at least 80 percent of the final dispositions that have been rendered in all identifiable child abuse crime cases in which there has been an event of activity within the last 5 years;

(B) continue to maintain a reporting rate of at least 80 percent for final dispositions in all identifiable child abuse crime cases in which there has been an event of activity within the preceding 5 years; and

(C) take steps to achieve 100 percent disposition reporting, including data quality audits and periodic notices to criminal justice agencies identifying records that lack final dispositions and requesting those disposition.

(c) LIASON.—An authorized agency of a State shall maintain close liaison with the National Center on Child Abuse and Neglect, the National Center for Missing and Exploited Children, and the National Center for the Prosecution of Child Abuse for the exchange of technical assistance in cases of child abuse.

(d) ANNUAL SUMMARY.—(1) The Attorney General shall publish an annual statistical summary of child abuse crimes.

(2) The annual statistical summary described in paragraph (1) shall not contain any

information that may reveal the identity of any particular victim or alleged violator.

(e) ANNUAL REPORT.—The Attorney General shall, subject to the availability of appropriations, publish an annual summary of each State's progress in reporting child abuse crime information to the national criminal history background check system.

(f) STUDY OF CHILD ABUSE OFFENDERS.—(1) Not later than 180 days after the date of enactment of this Act, the Administrator of the Office of Juvenile Justice and Delinquency Prevention shall begin a study based on a statistically significant sample of convicted child abuse offenders and other relevant information to determine—

(A) the percentage of convicted child abuse offenders who have more than 1 conviction for an offense involving child abuse;

(B) the percentage of convicted child abuse offenders who have been convicted of an offense involving child abuse in more than 1 State; and

(C) the extent to which and the manner in which instances of child abuse form a basis for convictions for crimes other than child abuse crimes.

(2) Not later than 1 year after the date of enactment of this Act, the Administrator shall submit a report to the Chairman of the Committee on the Judiciary of the Senate and the Chairman of the Committee on the Judiciary of the House of Representatives containing a description of and a summary of the results of the study conducted pursuant to paragraph (1).

SEC. 3. BACKGROUND CHECKS.

(a) IN GENERAL.—(1) A State may have in effect procedures (established by State statute or regulation) that require qualified entities designated by the State to contact an authorized agency of the State to request a nationwide background check for the purpose of determining whether a provider has been convicted of a crime that bears upon an individual's fitness to have responsibility for the safety and well-being of children.

(2) The authorized agency shall access and review State and Federal criminal history records through the national criminal history background check system and shall make reasonable efforts to respond to the inquiry within 15 business days.

(b) GUIDELINES.—The procedures established under subsection (a) shall require—

(1) that no qualified entity may request a background check of a provider under subsection (a) unless the provider first provides a set of fingerprints and completes and signs a statement that—

(A) contains the name, address, and date of birth appearing on a valid identification document (as defined in section 1028 of title 18, United States Code) of the provider.

(B) the provider has not been convicted of a crime and, if the provider has been convicted of a crime, contains a description of the crime and the particulars of the conviction;

(C) notifies the provider that the entity may request a background check under subsection (a);

(D) notifies the provider of the provider's right under paragraph (2); and

(E) notifies the provider that prior to the completion of the background check the qualified entity may choose to deny the provider unsupervised access to a child to whom the qualified entity provides child care;

(2) that each provider who is the subject of a background check is entitled —

(A) to obtain a copy of any background check report; and

(B) to challenge the accuracy and completeness of any information contained in any such report and obtain a prompt determination as to the validity of such challenge before a final determination is make by the authorized agency;

(3) that an authorized agency, upon receipt of a background check report lacking disposition data, shall conduct research in whatever State and local recordkeeping systems are available in order to obtain complete data;

(4) that the authorized agency shall make a determination whether the provider has been convicted of, or is under pending indictment for, a crime that bears upon an individual's fitness to have responsibility for the safety and well-being of children and shall convey that determination to the qualified entity; and

(5) that any background check under subsection (a) and the results thereof shall be handled in accordance with the requirements of Public Law 92-544.

(c) REGULATIONS. — (1) The Attorney General may by regulation prescribe such other measures as may be required to carry out the purposes of this Act, including measures relating to the security, confidentiality, accuracy, use, misuse, and dissemination of information, and audits and recordkeeping.

(2) The Attorney General shall, to the maximum extent possible, encourage the use of the best technology available in conducting background checks.

(d) LIABILITY. — A qualified entity shall not be liable in an action for damages solely for failure to conduct a criminal background check on a provider, nor shall a state or political subdivision thereof nor any agency, officer or employee thereof, be liable in an action for damages for the failure of a qualified entity to take action adverse to a provider who was the subject of a background check.

(e) FEES. — In the case of a background check pursuant to a State requirement adopted after the date of the enactment of this Act conducted with fingerprints on a person who volunteers with a qualified entity, the fees collected by authorized State agencies and the Federal Bureau of Investigation may not exceed the actual cost of the background check conducted with fingerprints. The States shall establish fee systems that insure that fees to non-profit entities for background checks do not discourage volunteers from participating in child care programs.

SEC. 4. FUNDING FOR IMPROVEMENT OF CHILD ABUSE CRIME INFORMATION.

(a) USE OF FORMULA GRANTS FOR IMPROVEMENTS IN STATE RECORDS AND SYSTEMS. — Section 509(b) of the Omnibus Crime Control and Safe Streets Act of 1968 (42 U.S.C. 3759(b)) is amended —

(1) in paragraph (2) by striking "and" after the semicolon;

(2) in paragraph (3) by striking the period and inserting "; and"; and

(3) by adding at the end the following new paragraph:

"(4) the improvement of State record systems and the sharing of all of the records described in paragraphs (1), (2), and (3) and the child abuse crime records required under the National Child Protection Act of 1993 with the Attorney General for the purpose of implementing the National Child Protection Act of 1993."

(b) ADDITIONAL FUNDING GRANTS FOR THE IMPROVEMENT OF CHILD ABUSE CRIME INFORMATION. — (1) The Attorney General shall, subject to appropriations and with preference to States that, as of the date of enactment of this Act, have in computerized criminal history files the lowest percentages of charges and dispositions of identifiable child abuse cases, make a grant to each State to be used—

(A) for the computerization of criminal history files for the purposes of this Act;

(B) for the improvement of existing computerized criminal history files for the purposes of this Act;

(C) to improve accessibility to the national criminal history background check system for the purposes of this Act; and

(D) to assist the State in the transmittal of criminal records to, or the indexing of criminal history record in, the national criminal history background check system for the purposes of this Act.

(2) There are authorized to be appropriated for grants under paragraph (1) a total of $20,000,000 for fiscal years 1994, 1995, 1996, and 1997.

(c) Withholding State Funds. — Effective 1 year after the date of enactment of this Act, the Attorney General may reduce, by up to 10 percent, the allocation to a State for a fiscal year under title I of the Omnibus Crime Control and Safe Streets Act of 1968 that is not in compliance with the requirements of this Act.

SEC. 5. DEFINITIONS.

For the purposes of this Act—

(1) the term "authorized agency" means a division or office of a State designated by a State to report, receive, or disseminate information under this Act;

(2) the term "child" means a person who is a child for purposes of the criminal child abuse law of a State;

(3) the term "child abuse crime" means a crime committed under any law of a State that involves the physical or mental injury, sexual abuse or exploitation, negligent treatment, or maltreatment of a child by any person;

(4) the term "child abuse crime information" means the following facts concerning a person who has been arrested for, or has been convicted of, a child abuse crime: full name, race, sex, date of birth, height, weight, fingerprints, a brief description of the child abuse crime or offenses for which the person has been arrested or has been convicted, the disposition of the charge, and any other information that the Attorney General determines may be useful in identifying persons arrested for, or convicted of, a child abuse crime;

(5) the term "child care" means the provision of care, treatment, education, training, instruction, supervision, or recreation to children by persons having unsupervised access to a child;

(6) the term "national criminal history background check system" means the criminal history record system maintained by the Federal Bureau of Investigation based on fingerprint identification or any other method of positive identification;

(7) the term "provider" means—

(A) a person who—

(i) is employed by or volunteers with a qualified entity;

(ii) who owns or operates a qualified entity; or

(iii) who has or may have unsupervised access to a child to whom the qualified entity provides child care; and

(B) a person who—

(i) seeks to be employed by or volunteer with a qualified entity;

(ii) seeks to own or operate a qualified entity; or

(iii) seeks to have or may have unsupervised access to a child to whom the qualified entity provides child care;

(8) the term "qualified entity" means a business or organization, whether public, private, for-profit, not-for-profit, or voluntary, that provides child care or child care placement services, including a business or organization that licenses or certifies others to provide child care or child care placement services; and

(9) the term "State" means a State, the District of Columbia, the Commonwealth of Puerto Rico, American Samoa, the Virgin Islands, Guam, and the Trust Territories of the Pacific.

Approved December 20, 1993.

Suggested Resources

General

Brock, Rita Nakashima. *Journeys by Heart: A Christology of Erotic Power*. New York: Crossroad, 1988.

Brown, Joanne Carlson, and Carole R. Bohn. *Christianity, Patriarchy and Abuse: A Feminist Critique*. NY: Pilgrim Press, 1989.

Cannon, Katie G. *Black Womanist Ethics*. Atlanta: Scholars Press, 1988.

Cleage, Pearl. *Mad at Miles: A Blackwoman's Guide to Truth*. Southfield, MI: The Cleage Group, Inc., 1989.

Cooper-White, Pamela. *The Cry of Tamar: Violence Against Women and the Church's Response*. Minneapolis: Fortress, 1995.

Doehring, Carrie. *Taking Care: Monitoring Power Dynamics and Relational Boundaries in Pastoral Care and Counseling*. Nashville: Abingdon, 1995.

Fiorenza, Elisabeth Schussler and Mary Shawn Copeland. *Violence Against Women*. Maryknoll, NY: Orbis, 1994.

Fortune, Marie. *Is Nothing Sacred: The Story of a Pastor, The Women He Sexually Abused, and the Congregation He Nearly Destroyed*. San Francisco: HarperSanFrancisco, 1989.

Fortune, Marie. *Love Does No Harm: Sexual Ethics for the Rest of Us*. New York: Continuum, 1995.

Herman, Judith. *Trauma and Recovery*. New York: Basic Books, 1992.

hooks, bell. *Sisters of the Yam: Black Women and Self-Recovery*. Boston: South End Press, 1993.

Jeffers, Susan. *Feel the Fear and Do It Anyway*. New York: Fawcett Columbine, 1987.

Poling, James Newton. *The Abuse of Power: A Theological Problem*. Nashville: Abingdon, 1991.

Poling, James Newton. *Deliver Us from Evil: Resisting Racial and Gender Oppression*. Minneapolis: Fortress, 1996.

Scott, Kesho Yvonne. *The Habit of Surviving: Black Women's Strategies for Life*. New Brunswick, NJ: Rutgers U. Press, 1991.

Stevens, Maryanne, ed. *Reconstructing the Christ Symbol: Essays in Feminist Christology*. New York: Paulist Press, 1993.

Townes, Emilie M. *Womanist Justice, Womanist Hope*. Atlanta: Scholars Press, 1993.

Townes, Emilie M. *A Troubling in My Soul: Womanist Perspectives on Evil and Suffering*. Maryknoll, New York: Orbis, 1993.

White, Evelyn. *The Black Women's Health Book: Speaking for Ourselves*. Seattle, WA: Seal Press, 1990.

White, Evelyn C. *Chain, Chain, Change: For Black Women Dealing with Physical and Emotional Abuse*. Seattle, WA: The Seal Press, 1985.

Child Abuse

Adams, Caren and Jennifer Fay. *No More Secrets: Protecting Your Child from Sexual Assault*. San Luis Obispo, CA: Impact Publishers, 1981.

Adams, Caren, Jennifer Fay and Jan Loreen-Martin. *No Is Not Enough: Helping Teenagers Avoid Sexual Assault*. San Louis Obispo, CA: Impact Publishers, 1984.

Bavolek, Stephen J. *A Handbook for Understanding Abuse and Neglect.* Park City, UT: Family Development Resources, Inc., 1990.

Brown, Joanne Carlson and Carole R. Bohn, eds. *Christianity, Patriarchy, and Abuse.* New York: Pilgrim Press, 1989.

Burdick, Faye, ed. *God's Plan for Growing Up: Amazing Stuff.* Louisville: Curriculum Publishing, Presbyterian Church (U.S.A.), 1996. Sexuality curriculum for grades 4–5.

Burdick, Faye, ed. *God's Plan for Growing Up: Wonderfully Made.* Louisville: Curriculum Publishing, Presbyterian Church (U.S.A.), 1996. Sexuality curriculum for grades 2–3.

Byerly, Carolyn M. *The Mother's Book: How to Survive the Molestation of Your Child.* Dubuque, IA: Kendall/Hunt Publishing Company, (Second Edition)1992.

Carlson, Lee W. *Child Sexual Abuse: A Handbook for Clergy and Church Members.* Valley Forge, PA: Judson Press, 1988.

Foote, Catherine J. *Survivor Prayers: Talking with God About Childhood Sexual Abuse.* Louisville: Westminster John Knox Press, 1996.

Fortune, Marie M. *Sexual Abuse Prevention: A Study for Teenagers.* Cleveland: United Church of Christ Press, 1984. Revised, 1996.

The Future of Children: Sexual Abuse of Children. Los Altos, CA: Center for the Future of Children, 1994.

God's Gift of Sexuality: A Study for Young People in the Reformed Tradition. Louisville: Curriculum Publishing, Presbyterian Church (U.S.A.), 1989. Sexuality curriculum for younger and older youth.

Guidelines for Child Care at Church-Sponsored Meetings. Published by the Presbyterian Child Advocacy Network, 1995. (PDC #72-650-95-002)

Heggen, Carolyn Holderread. *Sexual Abuse in Christian Homes and Churches.* Scottdale, PA: Herald Press, 1993.

Horton, Anne L. and Judith A. Williamson. *Abuse and Religion: When Praying Isn't Enough.* Lexington, MA: D. C. Heath and Co., 1988.

Mackey, Virginia. *Restorative Justice: A Discussion Paper on Crime and Justice.* Published by the Presbyterian Criminal Justice Program of the Presbyterian Church (U.S.A.), 1992. (PDC #258-92-706)

McDonald, Bonnie Glass. *Child Abuse Ministry: A Bibliography of Resources for the Religious Community.* New York: National Council of Churches, 1995.

McDonald, Bonnie Glass. *Surely Heed Their Cry: A Presbyterian Guide to Child Abuse Prevention, Intervention, and Healing.* Published by the Presbyterian Child Advocacy Network, 1993. (PDC #257-93-010)

Nelson, Mary and Kay Clark, eds. *The Educator's Guide to Preventing Child Sexual Abuse.* Santa Cruz, CA: Network Publications, 1986.

Pais, Janet. *Suffer the Children: A Theology of Liberation by a Victim of Child Abuse.* New York: Paulist Press, 1991.

Pellauer, Mary D., Barbara Chester, and Jane Boyajian. *Sexual Assault and Abuse: A Manual for Clergy and Religious Professionals.* San Francisco: Harper and Row, 1987.

Reid, Kathryn Goering. *Preventing Child Sexual Abuse: Ages 5–8.* Cleveland: United Church of Christ Press, 1994.

Reid, Kathryn Goering and Marie M. Fortune. *Preventing Child Sexual Abuse: Ages 9–12.* Cleveland: United Church of Christ Press, 1989.

Winters, Mary S., J.D. *Laws Against Sexual and Domestic Violence: A Concise Guide for Clergy and Laity.* New York: Pilgrim Press, 1988.

Welcome the Child: A Child Advocacy Guide for Churches. Produced by the Children's Defense Fund, 1990.

Videos

Bless Our Children: Preventing Sexual Abuse. Produced by the Center for the Prevention of Sexual and Domestic Violence, 936 N. 34th Street, Suite 200, Seattle, WA, 93103.

Hear Their Cries: Religious Responses to Child Abuse. Produced by the Center for the Prevention of Sexual and Domestic Violence, 936 N. 34th Street, Suite 200, Seattle, WA, 93103.

Reducing the Risk of Child Sexual Abuse in Your Church. Video and study guides produced by Church Law and Tax Report, Christian Ministry Resources, P. O. Box 1098, Matthews, NC 28106.

Acquaintance Rape/Date Rape

Estrich, Susan. *Real Rape.* Cambridge MA: Harvard U. Press, 1987.

Fellowship of Reconciliation Packet. *Actions for Compassion: Stop the War Against Women.* A packet for college women about violence against women. Available from Fellowship of Reconciliation, Box 271, Nyack, NY 10960, 914/358-4601.

Fortune, Marie Marshall. *Sexual Violence—The Unmentionable Sin: An Ethical and Pastoral Perspective.* New York: Pilgrim Press, 1983.

Keller, Daniel. *The Prevention of Rape and Sexual Assault on Campus.* Campus Crime Prevention Programs, P.O. Box 204, Goshen, KY 40026.

Levy, Barrie and Patricia Occhiuzzo Giggans. *What Parents Need to Know About Dating Violence.* Seattle, WA: Seal Press, 1995.

Parrot, Andrea. *Coping with Date Rape and Acquaintance Rape.* New York: Rose Publishing Group, 1988.

Pellauer, Mary, et al., eds. *Sexual Assault and Abuse: A Handbook for Clergy and Religious Professionals.* San Francisco: Harper & Row, 1987.

Pritchard, Carol. *Avoiding Rape On and Off Campus.* Wenonah, NJ: State College Publishing Co., 1985.

Sanday, Peggy Reeves. *Fraternity Gang Rape: Sex, Brotherhood, and Privilege on Campus.* New York: New York U. Press, 1990.

Warshaw, Robin. *I Never Called It Rape.* New York: Harper & Row, 1988.

Youngs, Sharon K. *Confronting Domestic Violence: Not Just for Adults.* Louisville: Curriculum Publishing, Presbyterian Church (U.S.A.), 1996.

Video

Date Rape. Available from: Rape Treatment Center, Santa Monica Hospital Medical Center, 1250 Sixteenth Street, Santa Monica, CA 90404. $50.00.

For more information, contact the following agencies:

Center for the Prevention of Sexual and Domestic Violence, 1914 North 34th Street, Suite 205, Seattle, WA 98103.

Center for Women Policy Studies, 2000 P St., NW, Suite 508, Washington, DC 20036.

Men's Anti-Rape Resource Center, P. O. Box 73559, Washington, DC 20056.

National Coalition Against Domestic Violence, P. O. Box 34103, Washington, DC 20043-4103. Or call 800/333-SAFE.

National Coalition Against Sexual Assault, 2428 Ontario Road, NW, Washington, DC 20009.

Spouse Abuse

Adams, Carol J. *Woman-Battering.* Minneapolis: Fortress Press, 1994.

Adams, Carol J. and Marie Fortune. *Violence Against Women and Children: A Theological Handbook.* New York: Continuum, 1995.

Fortune, Marie M. *Keeping the Faith: Questions and Answers for the Abused Woman.* San Francisco: Harper & Row, 1987.

Fortune, Marie M. *Sexual Violence, the Unmentionable Sin: An Ethical and Pastoral Perspective.* Cleveland: Pilgrim Press, 1983.

Fortune, Marie M. *Violence in the Family: A Workshop Curriculum for Clergy and Other Helpers.* Cleveland: Pilgrim Press, 1991.

Gaddis, Patricia Riddle. *Battered But Not Broken: Help for Abused Wives and Their Church Families.* Valley Forge: Judson Press, 1996.

Miller, Melissa A. *Family Violence: The Compassionate Church Responds.* Scottdale, PA: Herald Press, 1994.

"Under His Thumb: Violence Against Women." *Current Issues,* Adult Foundational Curriculum, Presbyterian Church (U.S.A.). Ed. Frank Hainer. Louisville: Curriculum Publishing, 1992–93.

Voelkel-Haugen, Rebecca and Marie M. Fortune. *Sexual Abuse Prevention: A Study for Teenagers.* New York: Pilgrim Press, 1996.

Video

Broken Vows: Religious Perspectives on Domestic Violence. Produced by the Center for the Prevention of Sexual and Domestic Violence, 936 N. 34th Street, Suite 200, Seattle, WA 98103.

Elder Abuse

Brody, E. M. "The Aging of the Family." *Annals of the American Academy of Political and Social Sciences* 43 (1978): 13–27.

Brody, E. M. "'Women in the Middle' and Family Help to Older People." *The Gerontologist* 21 (1981): 471–80.

Callahan, J. "Elder Abuse: Some Questions for Policymakers." *The Gerontologist* 28 (1988): 453–58.

Coyne, A. C., W. R. Reichman, and L. J. Berbig. "The Relationship Between Dementia and Elder Abuse." *American Journal of Psychiatry* 150 (1993): 643.

Douglass, R. L. and P. Ruby-Douglass. "Domestic Abuse and Neglect of the Elderly." In Warner, C. G. And Braen, G. R., eds. *Management of the Physically and Emotionally Abused: Emergency Assessment, Intervention and Counseling.* Norwalk, CT: Capistrano Press/Appelton-Century-Crofts, 1982.

Douglass, R. L. "Opportunities for Prevention of Domestic Neglect and Abuse of the Elderly." In Simson, S., et al., eds. *Aging and Prevention.* New York: Hayworth Press, 1983.

Fulmer, T. "Mistreatment of Elders, Assessment, Diagnosis, and Intervention." *Nurs Clin North Am* 24 (1989): 707.

Fulmer, T. "Clinical Assessment of Elder Abuse." In Fillinson R., and Ingman, S., eds., *Elder Abuse: Practice and Policy.* New York: Human Sciences Press, 1989.

Kutza, E. A. "Toward an Aging Policy." *Social Policy,* May–June, 1981, 39–43.

Palmore, E. *Social Patterns in Normal Aging.* Durham: Duke University Press, 1981.

Pillemer, Karl A. and D. Finkelhor. "The Prevalence of Elder Abuse: A Random Sample Survey." *The Gerontologist* 28 (1988): 51.

Pillemer, Karl A. And Rosalie S. Wolf, eds. *Elder Abuse: Conflict in the Family.* Dover, MA: Auburn House Publishing Co., 1986.

Quinn, Mary Joy and Susan K. Tomita. *Elder Abuse and Neglect: Causes, Diagnosis and Intervention Strategies.* New York: Springer Publishing Co., 1986.

Taler, G. and E. Ansello. "Elder Abuse." *American Family Physician* 32 (1985): 107–14.

Weiner, A. "A Community Based Education Model for Identification and Prevention of Elder Abuse." *Journal of Gerontological Social Work* 16 (1991): 107–119.

Weith, M. E. "Elder Abuse: A National Tragedy." *FBI Law Enforcement Bulletin* 63 (1994): 24–26.